studysync®

Reading & Writing Companion

In the Dark

How do you know what to do when there are no instructions?

studysync.com

Send all inquiries to:
BookheadEd Learning, LLC
610 Daniel Young Drive
Sonoma, CA 95476

ISBN 978-1-94-469575-0

1 2 3 4 5 6 QVS 24 23 22 21 20 19

A

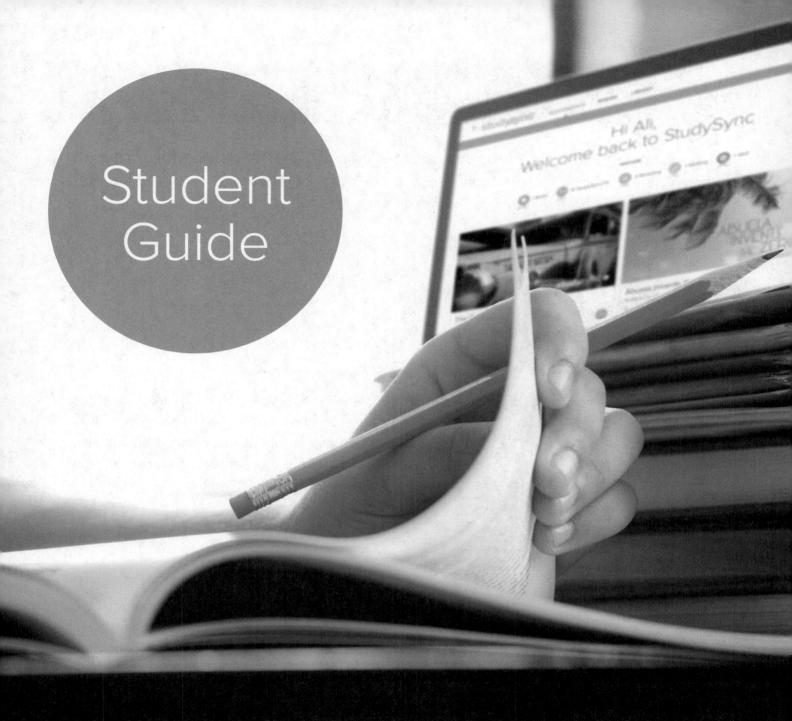

Student Guide

Getting Started

Welcome to the StudySync Reading & Writing Companion! In this book, you will find a collection of readings based on the theme of the unit you are studying. As you work through the readings, you will be asked to answer questions and perform a variety of tasks designed to help you closely analyze and understand each text selection. Read on for an explanation of each

Close Reading and Writing Routine

In each unit, you will read texts that share a common theme, despite their different genres, time periods, and authors. Each reading encourages a closer look through questions and a short writing assignment.

Eleven

FICTION
Sandra Cisneros
1991

Introduction   study**sync**●

Sandra Cisneros (b. 1954) is a renowned Chicana writer whose poems, novels, and short stories explore the complicated struggle of finding one's own identity. Cisneros is best known for her novel *The House on Mango Street* and the collection *Woman Hollering Creek and Other Stories*. "Eleven" is from the latter, the story of a girl named Rachel who experiences growing pains on her eleventh birthday. When her teacher insists that an ugly red sweater belongs to Rachel, the eleven-year-old has exceptional thoughts but can't share them. Even so, it's evident that the protagonist of Sandra Cisneros's short story has insight beyond her years.

Eleven

"You open your eyes and everything's just like yesterday, only it's today. And you don't feel eleven at all."

What they don't understand about birthdays and what they never tell you is that when you're eleven, you're also ten, and nine, and eight, and seven, and six, and five, and four, and three, and two, and one. And when you wake up on your eleventh birthday you expect to feel eleven, but you don't. You open your eyes and everything's just like yesterday, only it's today. And you don't feel eleven at all. You feel like you're still ten. And you are—underneath the year that makes you eleven.

Like some days you might say something stupid, and that's the part of you that's still ten. Or maybe some days you might need to sit on your mama's lap because you're scared, and that's the part of you that's five. And maybe one day when you're all grown up maybe you will need to cry like if you're three, and that's okay. That's what I tell Mama when she's sad and needs to cry. Maybe she's feeling three.

Because the way you grow old is kind of like an onion or like the rings inside a tree trunk or like my little wooden dolls that fit one inside the other, each year inside the next one. That's how being eleven years old is.

You don't feel eleven. Not right away. It takes a few days, weeks even, sometimes even months before you say Eleven when they ask you. And you don't feel smart eleven, not until you're almost twelve. That's the way it is.

Only today I wish I didn't have only eleven years rattling inside me like pennies in a tin Band-Aid box. Today I wish I was one hundred and two instead of eleven because if I was one hundred and two I'd have known what to say when Mrs. Price put the red sweater on my desk. I would've known how to tell her it wasn't mine instead of just sitting there with that look on my face and nothing coming out of my mouth.

"Whose is this?" Mrs. Price says, and she holds the red sweater up in the air for all the class to see. "Whose? It's been sitting in the coatroom for a month."

Skill: Figurative Language

The narrator uses similes when she compares aging to everyday things. When I picture onions, tree trunks, and wooden dolls, I notice they all have layers. She must mean that when you get older, you keep getting more layers.

Introduction ①

An Introduction to each text provides historical context for your reading as well as information about the author. You will also learn about the genre of the text and the year in which it was written.

Notes ②

Many times, while working through the activities after each text, you will be asked to **annotate** or **make annotations** about what you are reading. This means that you should highlight or underline words in the text and use the "Notes" column to make comments or jot down any questions you have. You may also want to note any unfamiliar vocabulary words here.

You will also see sample student annotations to go along with the Skill lesson for that text.

  Reading & Writing Companion

③ First Read

During your first reading of each selection, you should just try to get a general idea of the content and message of the reading. Don't worry if there are parts you don't understand or words that are unfamiliar to you. You'll have an opportunity later to dive deeper into the text.

④ Think Questions

These questions will ask you to start thinking critically about the text, asking specific questions about its purpose, and making connections to your prior knowledge and reading experiences. To answer these questions, you should go back to the text and draw upon specific evidence to support your responses. You will also begin to explore some of the more challenging vocabulary words in the selection.

⑤ Skills

Each Skill includes two parts: Checklist and Your Turn. In the Checklist, you will learn the process for analyzing the text. The model student annotations in the text provide examples of how you might make your own notes following the instructions in the Checklist. In the Your Turn, you will use those same instructions to practice the skill.

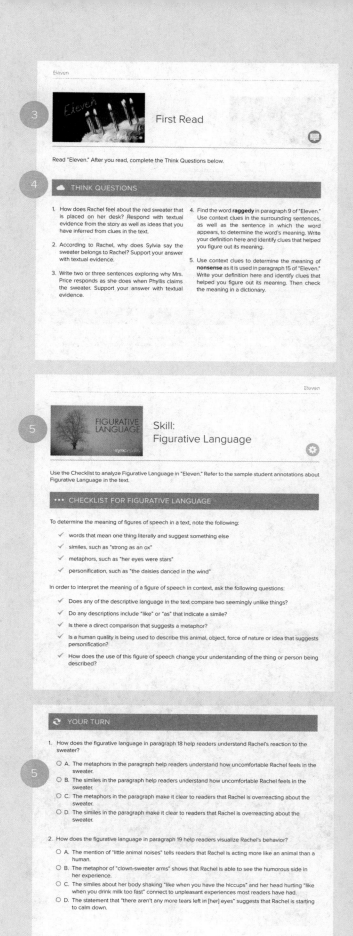

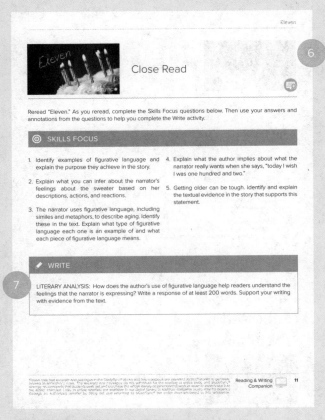

Close Read

Reread "Eleven." As you reread, complete the Skills Focus questions below. Then use your answers and annotations from the questions to help you complete the Write activity.

◎ SKILLS FOCUS

1. Identify examples of figurative language and explain the purpose they achieve in the story.

2. Explain what you can infer about the narrator's feelings about the sweater based on her descriptions, actions, and reactions.

3. The narrator uses figurative language, including similes and metaphors, to describe aging. Identify these in the text. Explain what type of figurative language each one is an example of and what each piece of figurative language means.

4. Explain what the author implies about what the narrator really wants when she says, "today I wish I was one hundred and two."

5. Getting older can be tough. Identify and explain the textual evidence in the story that supports this statement.

✏ WRITE

LITERARY ANALYSIS: How does the author's use of figurative language help readers understand the feelings that the narrator is expressing? Write a response of at least 200 words. Support your writing with evidence from the text.

Lost Island
FICTION

Introduction

Marina wakes up alone, thirsty, and hungry on a deserted island. How did she get here, and why is her head throbbing? As she slowly recalls a large wave smashing into Uncle Merlin's fishing boat, Marina takes her first steps towards survival.

▼ VOCABULARY

damp
wet

capsized
tipped over in the water

intense
very strong

rescuer
someone who saves a person from harm or danger

Close Read & Skills Focus

After you have completed the First Read, you will be asked to go back and read the text more closely and critically. Before you begin your Close Read, you should read through the Skills Focus to get an idea of the concepts you will want to focus on during your second reading. You should work through the Skills Focus by making annotations, highlighting important concepts, and writing notes or questions in the "Notes" column. Depending on instructions from your teacher, you may need to respond online or use a separate piece of paper to start expanding on your thoughts and ideas.

Write

Your study of each selection will end with a writing assignment. For this assignment, you should use your notes, annotations, personal ideas, and answers to both the Think and Skills Focus. Be sure to read the prompt carefully and address each part of it in your writing.

English Language Learner

The English Language Learner texts focus on improving language proficiency. You will practice learning strategies and skills in individual and group activities to become better readers, writers, and speakers.

Extended Writing Project

This is your opportunity to use genre characteristics and craft to compose meaningful, longer written works exploring the theme of each unit. You will draw information from your readings, research, and own life experiences to complete the assignment.

1 Writing Project

After you have read all of the unit text selections, you will move on to a writing project. Each project will guide you through the process of writing your essay. Student models will provide guidance and help you organize your thoughts. One unit ends with an **Extended Oral Project** which will give you an opportunity to develop your oral language and communication skills.

2 Writing Process Steps

There are four steps in the writing process: Plan, Draft, Revise, and Edit and Publish. During each step, you will form and shape your writing project, and each lesson's peer review will give you the chance to receive feedback from your peers and teacher.

3 Writing Skills

Each Skill lesson focuses on a specific strategy or technique that you will use during your writing project. Each lesson presents a process for applying the skill to your own work and gives you the opportunity to practice it to improve your writing.

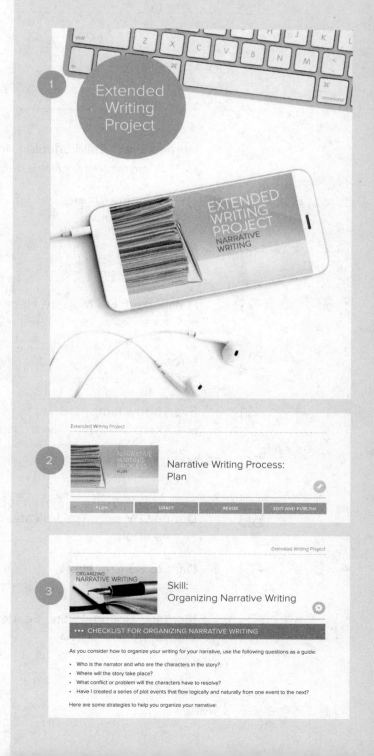

1 Extended Writing Project

EXTENDED WRITING PROJECT NARRATIVE WRITING

Extended Writing Project

2 Narrative Writing Process: Plan

PLAN | DRAFT | REVISE | EDIT AND PUBLISH

Extended Writing Project

3 Skill: Organizing Narrative Writing

••• CHECKLIST FOR ORGANIZING NARRATIVE WRITING

As you consider how to organize your writing for your narrative, use the following questions as a guide:

- Who is the narrator and who are the characters in the story?
- Where will the story take place?
- What conflict or problem will the characters have to resolve?
- Have I created a series of plot events that flow logically and naturally from one event to the next?

Here are some strategies to help you organize your narrative:

In the Dark

How do you know what to do when there are no instructions?

Genre Focus: INFORMATIONAL

Texts

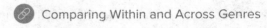 Comparing Within and Across Genres

Reading & Writing Companion

Extended Writing Project: Informative Writing

Unit 3: In the Dark

How do we know what to do when there are no instructions?

CARL HIAASEN

Carl Hiaasen (b. 1953) has been a regular columnist for the *Miami Herald* since 1985, reporting and commenting on everything from the Everglades to local politics to Facebook to raccoons. He has also written a number of novels for adults and for younger audiences, all set in Florida. In an interview with *Strand Magazine*, Hiassen stated, "Every writer's obligation is to create enough suspense to keep the readers turning the pages, and it's doubly hard if you're trying to make them laugh along the way."

LANGSTON HUGHES

The final line of the poem "I, Too," by Langston Hughes (1902 – 1967) is chiseled in the stone wall of the National Museum of African American History and Culture in Washington, DC: "I, too, am America." Hughes first wrote these words in 1926 as a young poet at the forefront of the Harlem Renaissance in New York. Through the lasting impact of his poems, Hughes continues to edify and give voice to the African American experience in the United States.

MADELEINE L'ENGLE

American author Madeleine L'Engle (1918–2007) is known primarily for her works of fiction for young adults, including the novels *A Wrinkle in Time* and *A Wind in the Door*. She also wrote poetry and memoir, and served a long career as a librarian in New York. In her acceptance speech for the 1963 Newbery Award, L'Engle commented on how she wrote such resonant, popular work, stating: "Most of what is best in writing isn't done deliberately."

HAMILTON WRIGHT MABIE

After a short time practicing law, Hamilton Wright Mabie (1846–1916) terminated his career as an attorney in 1879 to become an editor at a magazine called *The Outlook*, published weekly in New York City, where he worked alongside Theodore Roosevelt. The first of over thirty books he published in his lifetime was *Norse Stories Retold* (1882), which he later expanded on by writing versions of myths, fairy tales, heroes, and legends for children.

RANDALL MUNROE

From an early age, Randall Munroe (b. 1984) loved reading *Calvin and Hobbes*. Years later, he would himself become a cartoonist after earning a degree in physics and working at NASA. He is most famous for *xkcd*, a stick figure webcomic that draws on technology, math, and science for content. Munroe writes a blog called *What If?* (and has published a book by the same name) which answers questions sent in by fans of his comics, such as: what if a rainstorm dropped all of its water in a single giant drop?

RICK RIORDAN

When Rick Riordan (b. 1964) moved to San Francisco from his native San Antonio around the age of thirty, he began missing Texas so much he was compelled to write a story set in his home state. Not long after, his first book *Big Red Tequila* (1997) was published and his life as an author began. Riordan was a middle school teacher at the time, who transitioned into being a full-time writer when he started writing a popular series about Percy Jackson, a twelve-year-old boy who discovers he is the son of Poseidon.

Heroes Every Child Should Know: Perseus

FICTION
Hamilton Wright Mabie
1914

Introduction

Perseus, the son of a mortal woman, Danaë, and Zeus, the king of the gods, faced challenges from the day he was born. Locked in a wooden chest, the infant and his mother are set adrift in the sea. They wash up safely on a remote island, where a fisherman takes them in and Perseus grows into a fine, able-bodied young man. One fateful day, he is visited by the goddess Athene, who has chosen him for the task of killing her bitter enemy Medusa, the snake-haired Gorgon whose gaze turns a beholder to stone. Perseus is all too willing to take on the mission,

"It is better to die like a hero than to live like an ox in a stall."

NOTES

from Chapter I: Perseus

1   Then Athene smiled and said:

2   "Be patient, and listen; for if you forget my words, you will indeed die. You must go northward to the country of the Hyperboreans,[1] who live beyond the pole, at the sources of the cold north wind, till you find the three Grey Sisters, who have but one eye and one tooth between them. You must ask them the way to the Nymphs, the daughters of the Evening Star, who dance about the golden tree, in the Atlantic island of the west. They will tell you the way to the Gorgon,[2] that you may slay her, my enemy, the mother of monstrous beasts. Once she was a maiden as beautiful as morn, till in her pride she sinned a sin at which the sun hid his face; and from that day her hair was turned to vipers, and her hands to eagle's claws; and her heart was filled with shame and rage, and her lips with bitter venom; and her eyes became so terrible that whosoever looks on them is turned to stone; and her children are the winged horse and the giant of the golden sword; and her grandchildren are Echidna the witch-adder, and Geryon the three-headed tyrant, who feeds his herds beside the herds of hell. So she became the sister of the Gorgons, the daughters of the Queen of the Sea. Touch them not, for they are **immortal;** but bring me only Medusa's head."

2   "And I will bring it!" said Perseus; "but how am I to escape her eyes? Will she not freeze me too into stone?"

4   "You shall take this polished shield," said Athene, "and when you come near her look not at her yourself, but at her image in the brass; so you may strike her safely. And when you have struck off her head, wrap it, with your face turned away, in the folds of the goatskin on which the shield hangs. So you will bring it safely back to me, and win to yourself **renown,** and a place among the heroes who feast with the Immortals upon the peak where no winds blow."

5   Then Perseus said, "I will go, though I die in going. But how shall I cross the seas without a ship? And who will show me my way? And when I find her, how shall I slay her, if her scales be iron and brass?"

---

1. **Hyperboreans:** giants in Greek myth who lived in the extreme north.
2. **Gorgons:** three monster-women of Greek myth, the most famous of whom is Medusa

NOTES

6　Now beside Athene appeared a young man more light-limbed than the stag, whose eyes were like sparks of fire. By his side was a **scimitar** of diamond, all of one clear precious stone, and on his feet were golden sandals, from the heels of which grew living wings.

7　Then the young man spoke: "These sandals of mine will bear you across the seas, and over hill and dale like a bird, as they bear me all day long; for I am Hermes, the far-famed Argus-slayer, the messenger of the Immortals who dwell on Olympus."

8　Then Perseus fell down and worshipped, while the young man spoke again:

9　"The sandals themselves will guide you on the road, for they are divine and cannot stray; and this sword itself the Argus-slayer, will kill her, for it is divine, and needs no second stroke. Arise, and gird them on, and go forth."

10　So Perseus arose, and girded on the sandals and the sword.

11　And Athene cried, "Now leap from the cliff and be gone."

12　But Perseus **lingered**.

13　"May I not bid farewell to my mother and to Dictys? And may I not offer burnt offerings to you, and to Hermes the far-famed Argus-slayer, and to Father Zeus above?"

14　"You shall not bid farewell to your mother, lest your heart **relent** at her weeping. I will comfort her and Dictys until you return in peace. Nor shall you offer burnt offerings to the Olympians; for your offering shall be Medusa's head. Leap, and trust in the armour of the Immortals."

Skill:
Character

Perseus's thoughts show that he's afraid to leap from the cliff. He's embarrassed by his fear, but his desire for fame is stronger, so he leaps. This action brings him closer to the resolution when he will battle with Medusa.

15　Then Perseus looked down the cliff and shuddered; but he was ashamed to show his dread. Then he thought of Medusa and the renown before him, and he leapt into the empty air.

16　And behold, instead of falling he floated, and stood, and ran along the sky. He looked back, but Athene had vanished, and Hermes; and the sandals led him on northward ever, like a crane who follows the spring toward the Ister fens.

17　So Perseus started on his journey, going dry-shod over land and sea; and his heart was high and joyful, for the winged sandals bore him each day a seven days' journey. And he turned neither to the right hand nor the left, till he came to the Unshapen Land, and the place which has no name.

18　And seven days he walked through it on a path which few can tell, till he came to the edge of the everlasting night, where the air was full of feathers, and the soil was hard with ice; and there at last he found the three Grey Sisters, by the shore of the freezing sea, nodding upon a white log of

NOTES

driftwood, beneath the cold white winter moon; and they chanted a low song together, "Why the old times were better than the new."

19   There was no living thing around them, not a fly, not a moss upon the rocks. Neither seal nor sea gull dare come near, lest the ice should clutch them in its claws. The surge broke up in foam, but it fell again in flakes of snow; and it frosted the hair of the three Grey Sisters, and the bones in the ice cliff above their heads. They passed the eye from one to the other, but for all that they could not see; and they passed the tooth from one to the other, but for all that they could not eat; and they sat in the full glare of the moon, but they were none the warmer for her beams. And Perseus pitied the three Grey Sisters; but they did not pity themselves.

20   So he said, "Oh, venerable mothers, wisdom is the daughter of old age. You therefore should know many things. Tell me, if you can, the path to the Gorgon."

21   Then one cried, "Who is this who **reproaches** us with old age?" And another, "This is the voice of one of the children of men."

22   Then one cried, "Give me the eye, that I may see him"; and another, "Give me the tooth, that I may bite him." But Perseus, when he saw that they were foolish and proud, and did not love the children of men, left off pitying them. Then he stepped close to them, and watched till they passed the eye from hand to hand. And as they groped about between themselves, he held out his own hand gently, till one of them put the eye into it, fancying that it was the hand of her sister. Then he sprang back, and laughed, and cried:

23   "Cruel and proud old women, I have your eye; and I will throw it into the sea, unless you tell me the path to the Gorgon, and swear to me that you tell me right."

24   Then they wept, and chattered, and scolded; but in vain. They were forced to tell the truth, though, when they told it, Perseus could hardly make out the road.

25   "You must go," they said, "foolish boy, to the southward, into the ugly glare of the sun, till you come to Atlas the Giant, who holds the heaven and the earth apart. And you must ask his daughters, the Hesperides, who are young and foolish like yourself. And now give us back our eye, for we have forgotten all the rest."

26   So Perseus gave them back their eye. And he leaped away to the southward, leaving the snow and the ice behind. And the terns and the sea gulls swept laughing round his head, and called to him to stop and play, and the dolphins gambolled up as he passed, and offered to carry him on his back. And all night long the sea nymphs sang sweetly. Day by day the sun rose higher and leaped more swiftly into the sea at night, and more swiftly out of the sea at dawn; while Perseus skimmed over the billows like a sea gull, and his feet were never wetted; and leapt on from wave to wave, and his limbs were never weary, till he saw far away a mighty mountain, all rose-red in the setting

Skill:
Character

Perseus really is clever. He figures out what is going on with the Grey sisters and gains control of the eye.

He uses the eye as a way to get the information he wants in his quest to kill Medusa, which is the main conflict of the story.

I notice how Perseus has changed. He is brave and strong now. He is tough with the Grey sisters.

sun. Perseus knew that it was Atlas, who holds the heavens and the earth apart.

27 He leapt on shore, and wandered upward, among pleasant valleys and waterfalls. At last he heard sweet voices singing; and he guessed that he was come to the garden of the Nymphs, the daughters of the Evening Star. They sang like nightingales among the thickets, and Perseus stopped to hear their song; but the words which they spoke he could not understand. So he stepped forward and saw them dancing, hand in hand around the charmed tree, which bent under its golden fruit; and round the tree foot was coiled the dragon, old Ladon the sleepless snake, who lies there for ever, listening to the song of the maidens, blinking and watching with dry bright eyes.

28 Then Perseus stopped, not because he feared the dragon, but because he was bashful before those fair maids; but when they saw him, they too stopped, and called to him with trembling voices:

29 "Who are you, fair boy? Come dance with us around the tree in the garden which knows no winter, the home of the south wind and the sun. Come hither and play with us awhile; we have danced alone here for a thousand years, and our hearts are weary with longing for a playfellow."

30 "I cannot dance with you, fair maidens; for I must do the errand of the Immortals. So tell me the way to the Gorgon, lest I wander and perish in the waves."

31 Then they sighed and wept; and answered:

32 "The Gorgon! she will freeze you into stone."

33 "It is better to die like a hero than to live like an ox in a stall. The Immortals have lent me weapons, and they will give me wit to use them."

34 Then they sighed again and answered: "Fair boy, if you are bent on your own ruin, be it so. We know not the way to the Gorgon; but we will ask the giant Atlas above upon the mountain peak." So they went up the mountain to Atlas their uncle, and Perseus went up with them. And they found the giant kneeling, as he held the heavens and the earth apart.

35 They asked him, and he answered mildly, pointing to the sea board with his mighty hand, "I can see the Gorgons lying on an island far away, but this youth can never come near them, unless he has the hat of darkness, which whosoever wears cannot be seen."

36 Then cried Perseus, "Where is that hat, that I may find it?"

37 But the giant smiled. "No living mortal can find that hat, for it lies in the depths of Hades, in the regions of the dead. But my nieces are immortal, and they shall fetch it for you, if you will promise me one thing and keep your faith."

38   Then Perseus promised; and the giant said, "When you come back with the head of Medusa, you shall show me the beautiful horror, that I may lose my feeling and my breathing, and become a stone for ever; for it is weary labour for me to hold the heavens and the earth apart."

39   Then Perseus promised, and the eldest of the Nymphs went down, and into a dark cavern among the cliffs, out of which came smoke and thunder, for it was one of the mouths of hell.

40   And Perseus and the Nymphs sat down seven days and waited trembling, till the Nymph came up again; and her face was pale, and her eyes dazzled with the light for she had been long in the dreary darkness; but in her hand was the magic hat.

The Arming of Perseus

41   Then all the Nymphs kissed Perseus, and wept over him a long while; but he was only impatient to be gone. And at last they put the hat upon his head, and he vanished out of their sight.

42   But Perseus went on boldly, past many an ugly sight, far away into the heart of the Unshapen Land, till he heard the rustle of the Gorgons' wings and saw the glitter of their **brazen** talons; and then he knew that it was time to halt, lest Medusa should freeze him into stone.

43   He thought awhile with himself, and remembered Athene's words. He arose aloft into the air, and held the mirror of the shield above his head, and looked up into it that he might see all that was below him.

44   And he saw the three Gorgons sleeping. He knew that they could not see him, because the hat of darkness hid him; and yet he trembled as he sank down near them, so terrible were those brazen claws.

45   Two of the Gorgons were foul as swine, and lay sleeping heavily, with their mighty wings outspread; but Medusa tossed to and fro restlessly, and as she tossed Perseus pitied her. But as he looked, from among her tresses the vipers' heads awoke, and peeped up with their bright dry eyes, and showed their fangs, and hissed; and Medusa, as she tossed, threw back her wings and showed her brazen claws.

46   Then Perseus came down and stepped to her boldly, and looked steadfastly on his mirror, and struck with Herpe stoutly once; and he did not need to strike again.

NOTES

47   Then he wrapped the head in the goat-skin, turning away his eyes, and sprang into the air aloft, faster than he ever sprang before.

48   For Medusa's wings and talons rattled as she sank dead upon the rocks; and her two foul sisters woke, and saw her lying dead.

49   Into the air they sprang yelling, and looked for him who had done the deed. They rushed, sweeping and flapping, like eagles after a hare; and Perseus's blood ran cold as he saw them come howling on his track; and he cried, "Bear me well now, brave sandals, for the hounds of Death are at my heels!"

50   And well the brave sandals bore him, aloft through cloud and sunshine, across the shoreless sea; and fast followed the hounds of Death. But the sandals were too swift, even for Gorgons, and by nightfall they were far behind, two black specks in the southern sky, till the sun sank and he saw them no more.

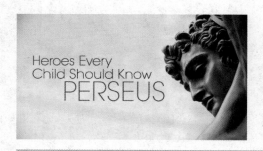

First Read

Read *Heroes Every Child Should Know: Perseus*. After you read, complete the Think Questions below.

☁ THINK QUESTIONS

1. How do Athene and Hermes help prepare Perseus for his journey? Cite textual evidence from the selection to support your answer.

2. Who else helps Perseus in his quest? How do they help him? Cite specific evidence from the text in your response.

3. How does Perseus feel about Medusa? Cite textual evidence from the selection to support your answer.

4. Find the word **renown** in paragraph 4 of "Heroes Every Child Should Know: Perseus." Use context clues in the surrounding sentences, as well as the sentence in which the word appears, to determine the word's meaning. Write your definition here and identify clues that helped you figure out its meaning.

5. Use context to determine the meaning of the word **scimitar** as it is used in the text. Write your definition here and identify clues that helped you figure out its meaning. Then check the meaning in a dictionary.

Skill:
Character

Use the Checklist to analyze Character in *Heroes Every Child Should Know: Perseus*. Refer to the sample student annotations about Character in the text.

••• CHECKLIST FOR CHARACTER

In order to determine how the characters respond or change as the plot moves toward a resolution, note the following:

- ✓ the characters in the story, including the protagonist and antagonist

- ✓ key events or series of episodes in the plot, especially events that cause characters to react, respond, or change in some way

- ✓ characters' responses as the plot reaches a climax, and moves toward a resolution of the problem facing the protagonist

- ✓ the resolution of the conflict in the plot and the ways that affects each character

- ✓ characters change or respond to events that move the plot toward a resolution

To describe how a particular story's or drama's plot unfolds in a series of episodes as well as how the characters respond or change as the plot moves toward a resolution, consider the following questions:

- ✓ How do the characters' responses change or develop from the beginning to the end of the story?

- ✓ Do the characters in the story change? Which event or events in the story causes a character to change?

- ✓ Is there an event in the story that provokes, or causes, a character to make a decision?

- ✓ Do the characters' problems reach a resolution? How?

- ✓ How does the resolution affect the characters?

- ✓ How do character's actions in response to events move the plot to a resolution?

Skill:
Character

Reread paragraphs 46–50 of *Heroes Every Child Should Know: Perseus*. Then, using the Checklist on the previous page, answer the multiple-choice questions below.

↻ YOUR TURN

1. Based on Perseus's actions in paragraphs 46 through 47, the reader can conclude that—

   ○ A. Athene will be pleased with the resolution of the plot's conflict.
   ○ B. Athene will be displeased with the resolution of the plot's conflict.
   ○ C. Hermes will be saddened over the resolution of the plot's conflict.
   ○ D. Hermes will be angry over the resolution of the plot's conflict.

2. When Perseus's blood runs cold in paragraph 49, it reveals that he has—

   ○ A. full confidence in Athene's plan.
   ○ B. no fear of death in the Unshapen Land.
   ○ C. brief doubt in Athene's plan.
   ○ D. no fear of Medusa's sisters.

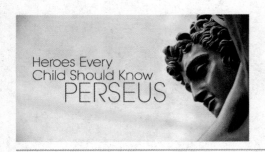

Close Read

Reread *Heroes Every Child Should Know: Perseus*. As you reread, complete the Skills Focus questions below. Then use your answers and annotations from the questions to help you complete the Write activity.

◎ SKILLS FOCUS

1. Many of Perseus's actions in his quest are prescribed by Athene. Identify one of his thoughts and one of his actions that surprise you. Then identify one of his responses that is not directed by Athene.

2. Identify actions of Perseus that reveal something about who he is and what he wants. Explain what the actions reveal.

3. Identify the resolution of the conflict in the story. Explain how this resolution contributes to the meaning of myth.

4. Identify textual evidence that indicates from what point of view the myth is told. Explain what the point of view is and how you know.

5. As he tells the Nymphs, Perseus is on an errand for the immortals. Identify situations in the quest that test Perseus's inner strength.

✏ WRITE

LITERARY ANALYSIS: How do Perseus's responses to individuals and events drive the action of the plot forward? Write a response of at least 300 words. Support your writing with evidence from the text.

The Lightning Thief

FICTION
Rick Riordan
2005

Introduction

studysync tv

Greek gods come to life in Rick Riordan's fantasy novel, *The Lightning Thief*. After being kicked out of boarding school, again, twelve-year-old Percy Jackson learns that his father is Poseidon, God of the Sea. Before long, Percy and his friends are off on a dangerous mission to find Zeus's missing lightning bolt, which must be returned before Mount Olympus erupts into war. Here, Percy questions his mother about the father who abandoned him, and then reflects on the odd things that seem to happen to him wherever he goes. This award-winning novel by Rick Riordan (b. 1964) has been adapted into a series of films. Riordan has also written other fictional series based on mythology, including *The Trials of Apollo* and *Magnus Chase and the Gods of Asgard*.

"... For your own good. I have to send you away."

NOTES

from Chapter 3

1 Our rental cabin was on the south shore, way out at the tip of Long Island. It was a little pastel box with faded curtains, half sunken into the dunes. There was always sand in the sheets and spiders in the cabinets, and most of the time the sea was too cold to swim in.

2 I loved the place.

3 We'd been going there since I was a baby. My mom had been going even longer. She never exactly said, but I knew why the beach was special to her. It was the place where she'd met my dad.

4 As we got closer to Montauk, she seemed to grow younger, years of worry and work disappearing from her face. Her eyes turned the color of the sea.

5 We got there at sunset, opened all the cabin's windows, and went through our usual cleaning routine. We walked on the beach, fed blue corn chips to the seagulls, and munched on blue jelly beans, blue saltwater taffy, and all the other free samples my mom had brought from work.

Skill: Story Structure

This flashback tells me that both Percy and his mother are rebellious. Percy admires his mom for not giving in to Gabe. This might be a clue that Percy is also not one to back down. It helps us learn more about the characters' personalities.

6 I guess I should explain about the blue food.

7 See, Gabe had once told my mom there was no such thing. They had this fight, which seemed like a really small thing at the time. But ever since, my mom went out of her way to eat blue. She baked blue birthday cakes. She mixed blueberry smoothies. She bought blue-corn tortilla chips and brought home blue candy from the shop. This—along with keeping her maiden name, Jackson, rather than calling herself Mrs. Ugliano—was proof that she wasn't totally suckered by Gabe. She did have a **rebellious** streak, like me.

8 When it got dark, we made a fire. We roasted hot dogs and marshmallows. Mom told me stories about when she was a kid, back before her parents died in the plane crash. She told me about the books she wanted to write someday, when she had enough money to quit the candy shop.

9 Eventually, I got up the nerve to ask about what was always on my mind whenever we came to Montauk—my father. Mom's eyes went all misty. I

NOTES

figured she would tell me the same things she always did, but I never got tired of hearing them.

10　"He was kind, Percy," she said. "Tall, handsome, and powerful. But gentle, too. You have his black hair, you know, and his green eyes."

11　Mom fished a blue jelly bean out of her candy bag. "I wish he could see you, Percy. He would be so proud."

12　I wondered how she could say that. What was so great about me? A **dyslexic, hyperactive** boy with a D+ report card, kicked out of school for the sixth time in six years.

13　"How old was I?" I asked. "I mean . . . when he left?"

14　She watched the flames. "He was only with me for one summer, Percy. Right here at this beach. This cabin."

15　"But . . . he knew me as a baby."

16　"No, honey. He knew I was expecting a baby, but he never saw you. He had to leave before you were born."

17　I tried to square that with the fact that I seemed to remember . . . something about my father. A warm glow. A smile.

18　I had always **assumed** he knew me as a baby. My mom had never said it outright, but still, I'd felt it must be true. Now, to be told that he'd never even seen me . . .

19　I felt angry at my father. Maybe it was stupid, but I **resented** him for going on that ocean voyage, for not having the guts to marry my mom. He'd left us, and now we were stuck with Smelly Gabe.

20　"Are you going to send me away again?" I asked her. "To another boarding school?"

21　She pulled a marshmallow from the fire.

22　"I don't know, honey." Her voice was heavy. "I think . . . I think we'll have to do something."

23　"Because you don't want me around?" I regretted the words as soon as they were out.

24　My mom's eyes welled with tears. She took my hand, squeezed it tight. "Oh, Percy, no. I—I *have* to, honey. For your own good. I have to send you away."

25　Her words reminded me of what Mr. Brunner had said—that it was best for me to leave Yancy.

26　"Because I'm not normal," I said.

Skill:
Story Structure

The word remember signals another flashback. Percy recalls something he associates with his father. But, Percy's mother suggests this memory is false. Maybe the story might be about Percy's missing dad.

27 "You say that as if it's a bad thing, Percy. But you don't realize how important you are. I thought Yancy Academy would be far enough away. I thought you'd finally be safe."

28 "Safe from what?"

29 She met my eyes, and a flood of memories came back to me—all the weird, scary things that had ever happened to me, some of which I'd tried to forget.

30 During third grade, a man in a black trench coat had stalked me on the playground. When the teachers threatened to call the police, he went away growling, but no one believed me when I told them that under his broad-brimmed hat, the man only had one eye, right in the middle of his head.

31 Before that—a really early memory. I was in preschool, and a teacher accidentally put me down for a nap in a cot that a snake had slithered into. My mom screamed when she came to pick me up and found me playing with a limp, scaly rope I'd somehow managed to strangle to death with my meaty toddler hands.

32 In every single school, something creepy had happened, something unsafe, and I was forced to move.

33 I knew I should tell my mom about the old ladies at the fruit stand, and Mrs. Dodds at the art museum, about my weird **hallucination** that I had sliced my math teacher into dust with a sword. But I couldn't make myself tell her. I had a strange feeling the news would end our trip to Montauk, and I didn't want that.

34 "I've tried to keep you as close to me as I could," my mom said. "They told me that was a mistake. But there's only one other option, Percy—the place your father wanted to send you. And I just . . . I just can't stand to do it."

35 "My father wanted me to go to a special school?"

36 "Not a school," she said softly. "A summer camp."

37 My head was spinning. Why would my dad—who hadn't even stayed around long enough to see me born—talk to my mom about a summer camp? And if it was so important, why hadn't she ever mentioned it before?

38 "I'm sorry, Percy," she said, seeing the look in my eyes. "But I can't talk about it. I—I couldn't send you to that place. It might mean saying good-bye to you for good."

39 "For good? But if it's only a summer camp . . ."

40 She turned toward the fire, and I knew from her **expression** that if I asked her any more questions she would start to cry.

Excerpted from *The Lightning Thief* by Rick Riordan, published by Miramax Books/Hyperion Books for Children.

First Read

Read *The Lightning Thief*. After you read, complete the Think Questions below.

 THINK QUESTIONS

1. How does Percy describe himself? Is his view of himself mostly positive or negative? Cite textual evidence from the selection to support your answer.

2. What's unusual about Percy's school attendance? Use details from the text in your response.

3. What does Percy discover about his father? How does this discovery make Percy feel? Cite textual evidence from the selection to support your answer.

4. Find the word **assumed** in paragraph 18 of *The Lightning Thief*. Use context clues in the surrounding sentences, as well as the sentence in which the word appears, to determine the word's meaning. Write your definition here and identify clues that helped you figure out its meaning.

5. Use context clues to determine the meaning of **resented** as it is used in paragraph 19 of *The Lightning Thief*. Write your definition here and identify clues that helped you figure out the meaning. Then check the meaning in a dictionary.

Skill:
Story Structure

Use the Checklist to analyze Story Structure in *The Lightning Thief*. Refer to the sample student annotations about Story Structure in the text.

••• CHECKLIST FOR STORY STRUCTURE

In order to identify how a particular sentence, chapter, scene or stanza fits into the overall structure of a text, note the following:

- ✓ the author's use of description, dialogue, and narration and how each develops the events of the plot

- ✓ the pattern the author uses to organize the events within a story or chapter

  - • chronological, or in time order
  - • events out of time order

- ✓ any literary devices the author uses, such as flashback, a part of a story that shows something that happened in the past

- ✓ any particular sentence, chapter, scene, or a stanza in a poem that contributes to the development of the setting, the plot, and the theme

- ✓ how a particular sentence, chapter, scene, or a stanza in a poem fits into the overall structure

To analyze how a particular sentence, chapter, scene, or stanza fits into the overall structure of a text and contributes to the development of the theme, setting, or plot, consider the following questions:

- ✓ What are the key events in the story and when did they take place?

- ✓ What impact does the order of events that take place in the story have on the theme, setting, or plot?

- ✓ What literary devices does the author use? How do they affect the development of the plot?

- ✓ How does a particular sentence, chapter, scene, or a stanza in a poem fit into the overall structure? How does it contribute to the development of the theme, setting, or plot?

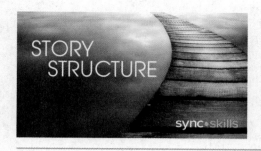

Skill:
Story Structure

Reread paragraphs 29–32 of *The Lightning Thief*. Then, using the Checklist on the previous page, answer the multiple-choice questions below.

♺ YOUR TURN

1. Which phrase from paragraph 29 best signals the author's use of flashback?

   ○ A. she met my eyes
   ○ B. flood of memories came back to me
   ○ C. weird, scary things
   ○ D. had ever happened to me

2. Why might the author choose to use the flashbacks in paragraphs 30 and 31?

   ○ A. to explain Percy's earlier anger toward his missing father
   ○ B. to describe Percy's mother's irrational fear that Percy isn't safe
   ○ C. to support Mr. Brunner's earlier claim that it's best for Percy to leave Yancy
   ○ D. to reinforce the idea that Percy is different and unique

3. Which sentence or phrase from the passage gives the clearest understanding that the story will be about Percy's struggles?

   ○ A. "She met my eyes, and a flood of memories came back to me. . ."
   ○ B. "In every single school, something creepy had happened, something unsafe, and I was forced to move."
   ○ C. "I was in preschool, and a teacher accidentally put me down for a nap in a cot that a snake had slithered into."
   ○ D. "My mom screamed when she came to pick me up and found me playing with a limp, scaly rope I'd somehow managed to strangle to death with my meaty toddler hands.

Close Read

Reread *The Lightning Thief*. As you reread, complete the Skills Focus questions below. Then use your answers and annotations from the questions to help you complete the Write activity.

◎ SKILLS FOCUS

1. Explain how the author's use of flashbacks about Percy's childhood help develop the plot.

2. Identify examples of Percy's thoughts that reveal how he feels about himself. Explain how these thoughts help establish Percy as an outsider.

3. Identify textual evidence that illustrates how the author uses dialogue between Percy and his mother to develop the plot and theme. Explain your reasoning.

4. In the ninth paragraph, Percy finally gets up the nerve to ask about his father. How is this an example of a turning point in the story, and how does it further develop the plot? Explain your reasoning.

5. Percy has many challenges and few instructions on how to resolve them. Identify evidence of these challenges and explain how they contribute to the story's conflict.

✏ WRITE

DISCUSSION: How does this excerpt from *The Lightning Thief* connect to the overall structure of the story? What hints does the author provide about the overall plot and theme? Think about how the author uses flashbacks to describe Percy's past, Percy's thoughts, and Percy's dialogue with his mother. As you prepare for your discussion, be sure to find plenty of textual evidence to support your ideas.

Elena

POETRY
Pat Mora
1994

Introduction

Pat Mora (b. 1942) is a celebrated Mexican American author whose bilingual works explore themes of culture and identity in families across Texas and along the Southwestern border, where Mora was born and raised. The poem presented here, "Elena," is told from the perspective of a mother who has emigrated from Mexico to the United States with her husband and their children. After some time in the States, her kids have adapted and now speak English even at home—a language in which the mother has little fluency. In direct and confessional language, the mother worries about the increasing cultural divide between her and her children

"I stand at the stove and feel dumb, alone."

NOTES

1 My Spanish isn't good enough.
2 I remember how I'd smile
3 listening to my little ones,
4 understanding every word they'd say,
5 their jokes, their songs, their **plots.**
6 *Vamos a pedirle dulces a mamá. Vamos.*
7 But that was in Mexico.
8 Now my children go to American high schools.
9 They speak English. At night they sit around
10 the kitchen table, laugh with one another.
11 I stand at the stove and feel dumb, alone.
12 I bought a book to learn English.
13 My husband **frowned**, drank more beer.
14 My oldest said, "*Mamá*, he doesn't want you
15 to be smarter than he is." I'm forty,
16 **embarrassed** at **mispronouncing** words,
17 embarrassed at the laughter of my children,
18 the grocer, the mailman. Sometimes I take
19 my English book and lock myself in the bathroom,
20 say the thick words softly,
21 for if I stop trying, I will be **deaf**
22 when my children need my help.

"Elena" from "Chants" by Pat Mora (©1994 Arte Público Press - University of Houston)

✏ WRITE

POEM: The poem "Elena" is told from the mother's point of view. Write a poem in response to the mother from the perspective of one of her children.

Hatshepsut: His Majesty, Herself

INFORMATIONAL TEXT
Catherine M. Andronik
2001

Introduction

In Egypt's eighteenth dynasty, during the mid-to-late 1400s BCE, a long pattern of male dominance was interrupted when Hatshepsut, the widow of Pharaoh Tuthmosis II, and daughter of the previous pharaoh, Tuthmosis I, took the throne. Hatshepsut's reign lasted 22 years, during which time she built great monuments, sent an expedition to the little-known land of Punt, and handed over a peaceful Egypt to her nephew, Tuthmosis III, who subsequently attempted to erase Hatshepsut's historical imprint.

"Hatshepsut took a bold and unprecedented step: She had herself crowned pharaoh . . ."

NOTES

1   Hatshepsut, royal daughter of **Pharaoh** Tuthmosis and his Great Wife Ahmose, grew up in an Egypt that was peaceful, **prosperous,** and respected throughout the known world.

2   Despite this prosperity, all but one of Hatshepsut's siblings died. Fatal diseases were common, deadly creatures such as scorpions flourished in the Egyptian desert, accidents happened, and a doctor's treatment was often more superstitious than scientific. When the time came for Pharaoh Tuthmosis to name an **heir** to his throne, only one son remained: Tuthmosis, son of Mutnofret, a woman of the pharaoh's harem. When he became pharaoh, young Tuthmosis would have little choice but to marry a woman of the royal blood. Marriages between close relatives were customary within ancient Egypt's royal family, so Hatshepsut was destined to become her half brother's wife. As the sole child of the pharaoh and the God's Wife, Hatshepsut was her dynasty's last hope to keep the royal bloodlines of Egypt intact.

Skill: Informational Text Elements

I notice that the author introduces the character Hatshepsut through an anecdote about her marrying her half-brother. That seems weird to me that Hatshepsut would have to marry her half-brother, but the author explains that this was "customary," or normal, in ancient Egypt. Plus, she really didn't have a choice. Hatshepsut was her family's last hope to keep the family as royalty.

3   Hatshepsut's father, Pharaoh Tuthmosis I, died at the relatively old age of of fifty. His secret tomb, the first underground chamber to be hidden in the towering cliffs of the Valley of the Kings, just northwest of Thebes,[1] had been excavated years in advance. The fine sarcophagus (sar-KOFF-ah-guss), or stone coffin, which would hold his body, was also ready. The pharaoh's mummy was carefully prepared, as befitted a great and beloved king. After seventy days, with solemn ceremony, Tuthmosis was laid in a tomb filled with all the choice food and drink, games and furniture, clothing and jewelry, and the little clay servant figures, called shawabtis (shah-WAHB-tees), that he could possibly need in the afterlife.

4   Following her father's death, Hatshepsut married her half brother, and the young man was crowned Pharaoh Tuthmosis II. Hatshepsut may have been only about twelve years old. As queen, she received a variety of new titles. Her favorite was God's Wife. Tuthmosis II and Hatshepsut had one child, a daughter named Neferure (neh-feh-Roo-ray).

5   The reign of Tuthmosis II was unremarkable. It was also brief, for he was a sickly young man. Within a few years of his coronation, Hatshepsut's husband had died.

---

1. **Thebes:** a Greek city important in ancient myth, home of Oedipus

6   With the death of Tuthmosis II, Egypt was left without a king to ensure that the many gods would look kindly upon the fragile desert land. *Maat* was a delicate thing, and without a pharaoh to tend to its preservation, it was in danger of collapsing.

7   Although Hatshepsut had been Tuthmosis II's Great Wife, he'd had other wives in his harem,[2] including one named Isis. Isis had borne the pharaoh a baby boy, who was also named Tuthmosis. Since Isis was not royal, neither was her baby. But like his father, he could grow up to be pharaoh if he married a princess of the royal blood: his half sister, Neferure.

8   Until Tuthmosis III was mature enough to be crowned pharaoh, what Egypt needed was a regent,[3] an adult who could take control of the country. The regent would have to be someone familiar with palace life and **protocol**. He would need to conduct himself with the proper authority around the royal advisors. He should be prepared to wield power if it became necessary, and he should feel comfortable around visiting dignitaries from other lands. He needed to know his place among the priests of the various gods.

9   It was a job Hatshepsut, perhaps just fifteen years old, had been training for since her earliest days by her father's side. Women had acted as regents for infants at other times in Egypt's history, and the gods had not frowned upon them.

10 So until Tuthmosis III was ready to be crowned as pharaoh, the acting ruler of Egypt would be his aunt, the royal widow of the king, Hatshepsut.

11 At first, little Tuthmosis III was considered the pharaoh, with Hatshepsut just his second-in-command. But a small child could not be an effective ruler. As Hatshepsut settled into her role as regent, she gradually took on more and more of the royal decision-making. She appointed officials and advisors; dealt with the priests; appeared in public ceremonies first behind, then beside, and eventually in front of her nephew. Gradually, over seven years, her power and influence grew. In the end, Hatshepsut was ruling Egypt in all but name.

12 There is no reliable record of exactly when or how it happened, but at some point, Hatshepsut took a bold and unprecedented step: She had herself crowned pharaoh with the large, heavy, red-and-white double crown of the two Egypts, north and south. Since all pharaohs took a throne name, a sort of symbolic name, upon their coronation, Hatshepsut chose Maatkare (maht-KAH-ray). *Maat,* that crucial cosmic order, was important to Hatshepsut. Egypt required a strong pharaoh to ensure *maat*. Hatshepsut could be that pharaoh—even if she did happen to be a woman.

---

2. **harem:** a household of wives and/or servants attached to one man
3. **regent:** a person who exercises power temporarily on behalf of a ruler or monarch

Skill: Central or Main Idea

These details support the main idea. Not only was Hatshepsut a female leader, she was a great, strong, female leader! She stood out from other women who had lead in the past.

NOTES

Skill: Informational Text Elements

Hatshepsut is trying hard to be like a man in order to keep up with tradition and please her people. She even dresses like a man and is called "pharaoh," or king. I think this shows that she is determined.

13 A few women had tried to rule Egypt before, but never with such a valid claim to the throne or at such a time of peace and prosperity. When Queens Nitocris and Sobekneferu had come to the throne in earlier dynasties, Egypt had been suffering from political problems, and there had been no male heirs. These women had not ruled long or well, and neither had had the audacity to proclaim herself pharaoh. Hatshepsut would be different.

14 There was no word in the language of ancient Egypt for a female ruler; a queen was simply the wife of a king. Hatshepsut had no choice: she had to call herself pharaoh, or king—a male title. She was concerned with preserving and continuing traditional order as much as possible, so to the people of Egypt she made herself look like a man in her role as pharaoh. In ceremonies, she wore a man's short kilt instead of a woman's long dress, much as she had as a child. Around her neck she wore a king's broad collar. She even fastened a false golden beard to her chin. When she wrote about herself as pharaoh, sometimes she referred to herself as he, other times as she. This would be very confusing for historians trying to uncover her identity thousands of years later.

15 Since Hatshepsut could not marry a queen, her daughter Neferure acted as God's Wife in public rituals. It was good training for Neferure, who would in time be expected to marry her half brother, Tuthmosis III, and be his royal consort. But Hatshepsut never seems to have considered that her daughter could succeed her as pharaoh.

16 Hatshepsut might have had to look and act like a man in public, but she never gave up feminine pleasures. Archaeologists have uncovered bracelets and alabaster cosmetic pots with Hatshepsut's cartouche (kar-TOOSH), or hieroglyphic name symbol, inscribed on each. Both men and women in Egypt used cosmetics. They needed creams and oils to keep their skin and hair from drying out under the brutal desert sun. And the kohl, a kind of makeup made from powdered lead that people applied around their eyes, did more than make them attractive; it also helped block out the sun's glare. But Hatshepsut was especially particular about her appearance. One inscription describes her as "more beautiful than anything."

17 With the exception of one military campaign against Nubia, Hatshepsut's reign was peaceful. Instead of expanding Egypt's borders through war and conquest, Hatshepsut built monuments within her country to proclaim its power. Her masterpiece was the magnificent temple at the site known today as Deir el-Bahri. The temple was dedicated to Amen, the

The Temple of Hetshepsut in the Valley of the Kings

god who was supposed to be the divine father of every pharaoh, the god to whom Hatshepsut felt she owed her good fortune. The temple at Deir el-Bahri was said to be Hatshepsut's own mortuary temple. The building is set into the side of a mountain and rises gracefully in three beautifully proportioned tiers, each supported by columns like those to be seen centuries later in Greek temples. Its design was far ahead of its time. Hatshepsut called it Djeser-Djeseru (JEH-sir jeh-SEH-roo)—"Holy of Holies."

18 On the walls of this temple, Hatshepsut had artists carve and paint her biography. According to the story told on the walls of Djeser-Djeseru, she had been chosen as pharaoh by the gods themselves, even before her birth. Perhaps, even after years on the throne, she still felt a need to **justify** a woman's right to rule. The gods in the pictures on the temple walls do not seem to care whether Hatshepsut is a man or a woman—in fact, some of the paintings show her as a boy.

Please note that excerpts and passages in the StudySync® library and this workbook are intended as touchstones to generate interest in an author's work. The excerpts and passages do not substitute for the reading of entire texts, and StudySync® strongly recommends that students seek out and purchase the whole literary or informational work in order to experience it as the author intended. Links to online resellers are available in our digital library. In addition, complete works may be ordered through an authorized reseller by filling out and returning to StudySync® the order form enclosed in this workbook.

Reading & Writing Companion 25

First Read

Read "Hatshepsut: His Majesty, Herself." After you read, complete the Think Questions below.

☁ THINK QUESTIONS

1. Before Hatshepsut became pharaoh, what experience does the text say she had for the job? Include evidence from the text to support your answer.

2. How was Hatshepsut's reign different from the reigns of the two earlier queens who had ruled Egypt? Use evidence from the text to support your answer.

3. What evidence does the text give to support the idea that Hatshepsut cared about her appearance? Refer to details from the text in your response.

4. Remembering that the Latin suffix -ous means "having, characterized by," use the context clues provided in the passage to determine the meaning of **prosperous**. Write your definition of "prosperous" here and tell how you were able to figure it out. In your answer, identify any relationships between words that helped you understand the meaning of "prosperous."

5. Use context to determine the meaning of the word **protocol** as it is used in the text. Then write your definition of *protocol* here and explain how you discovered the meaning of the word.

Skill:
Informational Text Elements

Use the Checklist to analyze Informational Text Elements in "Hatshepsut: His Majesty, Herself." Refer to the sample student annotations about Informational Text Elements in the text.

••• CHECKLIST FOR INFORMATIONAL TEXT ELEMENTS

In order to identify a key individual, event, or idea in a text, note the following:

- ✓ examples that describe or explain important ideas, events, or individuals in the text

- ✓ anecdotes in the text. An anecdote is a personal story an author has passed on to readers

- ✓ how a key individual, event, or idea is introduced or illustrated

- ✓ other features, such as charts, maps, sidebars, and photos that might provide additional information outside of the main text

To analyze in detail how a key individual, event, or idea is introduced, illustrated, and elaborated in a text, consider the following questions:

- ✓ How does the author introduce or illustrate a key individual, event, or idea?

- ✓ What key details does the author include to describe or elaborate on important information in the text?

- ✓ Does the author include any anecdotes? What do they add to the text?

- ✓ What other features, if any, help readers to analyze the events, ideas, or individuals in the text?

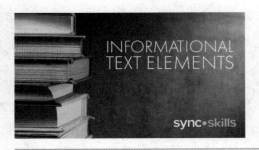

Skill:
Informational Text Elements

Reread paragraph 16 from "Hatshepsut: His Majesty, Herself." Then, using the Checklist on the previous page, answer the multiple-choice questions below.

⟳ YOUR TURN

1. This question has two parts. First, answer Part A. Then, answer Part B.

Part A: What does this paragraph reveal about Hatshepsut as an individual?

- ○ A. She was obsessed with her looks.
- ○ B. She was tired of acting like a man.
- ○ C. She was true to herself in private.
- ○ D. She hid her true gender from her people.

Part B: Which of the following details from the text best supports your answer to Part A?

- ○ A. "Hatshepsut might have had to look and act like a man in public, but she never gave up feminine pleasures."
- ○ B. "Archaeologists have uncovered bracelets and alabaster cosmetic pots with Hatshepsut's cartouche. . ."
- ○ C. "They needed creams and oils to keep their skin and hair from drying out under the brutal desert sun."
- ○ D. "One inscription describes her as 'more beautiful than anything.'"

2. Why does the author write that "both men and women in Egypt used cosmetics"?

    ○ A. to explain why Hatshepsut used cosmetics both in public and in private

    ○ B. to highlight an opinion concerning the use of cosmetics in ancient Egypt

    ○ C. to provide a factual detail that illustrates what ancient Egypt was like

    ○ D. to emphasize the anecdote about Hatshepsut and why she chose to dress like a man in public

Please note that excerpts and passages in the StudySync® library and this workbook are intended as touchstones to generate interest in an author's work. The excerpts and passages do not substitute for the reading of entire texts, and StudySync® strongly recommends that students seek out and purchase the whole literary or informational work in order to experience it as the author intended. Links to online resellers are available in our digital library. In addition, complete works may be ordered through an authorized reseller by filling out and returning to StudySync® the order form enclosed in this workbook.

Reading & Writing
Companion

29

Skill:
Central or Main Idea

Use the Checklist to analyze Central or Main Idea in "Hatshepsut: His Majesty, Herself." Refer to the sample student annotations about Central or Main Idea in the text.

••• CHECKLIST FOR CENTRAL OR MAIN IDEA

In order to identify a central idea of a text, note the following:

- ✓ the topic or subject of the text

- ✓ the central or main idea, if it is explicitly stated

- ✓ details in the text that convey the theme

To determine a central idea of a text and how it is conveyed through particular details consider the following questions:

- ✓ What main idea do the details in one or more paragraphs explain or describe?

- ✓ What bigger idea do all the paragraphs support?

- ✓ What is the best way to state the central idea? How might you summarize the text and message?

- ✓ How do particular details in the text convey the central idea?

Skill:
Central or Main Idea

Reread paragraph 17 from "Hatshepsut: His Majesty, Herself." Then, using the Checklist on the previous page, answer the multiple-choice questions below.

 YOUR TURN

1. This question has two parts. First, answer Part A. Then, answer Part B.

Part A: Which of the following statements best portrays the central idea of the paragraph?

- ○ A. Hatshepsut ensured violent military operations through which she was able to keep the peace.
- ○ B. Hatshepsut successfully built temples throughout Egypt, thus pleasing her people.
- ○ C. Hatshepsut's use of dynamic temple designs blazed a trail for future leaders.
- ○ D. Hatshepsut successfully led Egypt by exercising peaceful tactics to maintain power.

Part B: Which detail from the paragraph best supports your answer to Part A?

- ○ A. "With the exception of one military campaign against Nubia, Hatshepsut's reign was peaceful."
- ○ B. "Instead of expanding Egypt's borders through war and conquest, Hatshepsut built monuments within her country to proclaim its power."
- ○ C. "Her masterpiece was the magnificent temple at the site known today as Deir el-Bahri."
- ○ D. "The building is set into the side of a mountain and rises gracefully in three beautifully proportioned tiers . . ."

Please note that excerpts and passages in the StudySync® library and this workbook are intended as touchstones to generate interest in an author's work. The excerpts and passages do not substitute for the reading of entire texts, and StudySync® strongly recommends that students seek out and purchase the whole literary or informational work in order to experience it as the author intended. Links to online resellers are available in our digital library. In addition, complete works may be ordered through an authorized reseller by filling out and returning to StudySync® the order form enclosed in this workbook.

Reading & Writing Companion 31

Close Read

Reread "Hatshepsut: His Majesty, Herself." As you reread, complete the Skills Focus questions below. Then use your answers and annotations from the questions to help you complete the Write activity.

◎ SKILLS FOCUS

1. Find evidence that supports the author's main idea in "Hatshepsut: His Majesty, Herself." Explain how this evidence supports the main idea.

2. Identify at least two informational text elements (such as anecdotes or examples) that introduce, illustrate, or elaborate the life of the pharaoh Hatshepsut.

3. Identify evidence of Hatshepsut's leadership skills and explain how you would restate the main ideas and the most important details of the text in your own words.

4. The Essential Question asks: "How do we know what to do when there are no instructions?" Identify evidence in "Hatshepsut: His Majesty, Herself" that reveals how Hatshepsut made history by breaking tradition.

✏ WRITE

ARGUMENTATIVE: In "Elena," a woman strives to learn English in order to benefit her children, despite her family's lack of support. Similarly, in "Hatshepsut: His Majesty, Herself," a woman defies all odds and many years of tradition by becoming a pharaoh in Egypt to benefit her family and keep their royal lineage intact. Keeping these women in mind, respond to the following prompt: What central or main idea does the author of "Hatshepsut: His Majesty, Herself" convey about female empowerment? In your response, use evidence from the text to support your claim.

I, Too

POETRY
Langston Hughes
1925

Introduction

Born in Joplin, Missouri, James Mercer Langston Hughes (1902–1967) was an influential figure during the Harlem Renaissance, where he helped pioneer a new literary art form called jazz poetry. Inspired by Carl Sandburg and Walt Whitman, Hughes wrote poems that gave voice to his own experiences and the shared experiences of other African Americans during the era of segregation. "I, Too" starts as a personal statement and extends to inspire future generations

"I, too, am America."

NOTES

Skill: Poetic Elements and Structure

The speaker says he is the "darker brother." I think this means he is black. But by calling himself "brother" he must mean that he is still in some way connected to the people who send him to eat in the kitchen.

Skill: Media

The audio version of the poem emphasizes the speaker's upbeat tone. He has a sing-song tone to his voice when he speaks these lines. I think this is because he knows that change is coming and that he will be considered equal.

1   I, too, sing America.

2   I am the **darker** brother.
3   They send me to eat in the kitchen
4   When **company** comes,
5   I laugh,
6   And eat well,
7   And grow strong.

8   **Tomorrow**,
9   I'll be at the table
10 When company comes.
11 Nobody'll **dare**
12 Say to me,
13 "Eat in the kitchen,"
14 Then.

15 Besides,
16 They'll see how beautiful I am
17 And be **ashamed** —

18 I, too, am America.

"I, Too" from THE COLLECTED POEMS OF LANGSTON HUGHES by Langston Hughes, edited by Arnold Rampersad with David Roessel, Associate Editor, copyright © 1994 by the Estate of Langston Hughes. Used by permission of Alfred A. Knopf, an imprint of the Knopf Doubleday Publishing Group, a division of Random House LLC. All rights reserved.

By permission of Harold Ober Associates Incorporated.
Copyright © 1994 by The Estate of Langston Hughes.

First Read

Read "I, Too, Sing America." After you read, complete the Think Questions below.

1. Who is the speaker of the poem? How do you know? Refer to one or more details from the beginning of the text to support your response.

2. What is the speaker comparing in lines 2–4 and 8–10? How are these two sets of lines similar? How are they different? Cite specific evidence from the text to support your answer.

3. Why will those who make the speaker "eat in the kitchen," in line 3, "be ashamed" in the future? Cite specific evidence from the text to support your response.

4. Read the following dictionary entry:

com•pa•ny \kəmp(ə)nē\ *noun*

    a A business or other commercial organization
    b. A visiting person or group
    c. A group of soldiers

Which definition most closely matches the meaning of **company** as it is used in line 4? Write the correct definition of *company* here and explain how you figured out the correct meaning.

5. Based on the context of the poem, what do you think the word **dare** means in line 11? Write your definition of *dare* here and confirm the meaning in a print or digital dictionary.

Please note that excerpts and passages in the StudySync® library and this workbook are intended as touchstones to generate interest in an author's work. The excerpts and passages do not substitute for the reading of entire texts, and StudySync® strongly recommends that students seek out and purchase the whole literary or informational work in order to experience it as the author intended. Links to online resellers are available in our digital library. In addition, complete works may be ordered through an authorized reseller by filling out and returning to StudySync® the order form enclosed in this workbook.

Reading & Writing Companion 35

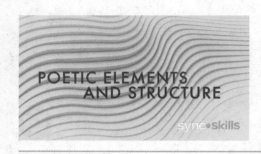

Skill:
Poetic Elements and Structure

Use the Checklist to analyze Poetic Elements and Structure in "I, Too, Sing America." Refer to the sample student annotations about Poetic Elements and Structure in the text.

••• CHECKLIST FOR POETIC ELEMENTS AND STRUCTURE

In order to identify elements of poetic elements and structure, note the following:

- ✓ how the words and lines are arranged

- ✓ the form and overall structure of the poem

- ✓ the rhyme, rhythm, and meter, if present

- ✓ how the arrangement of lines and stanzas in the poem contribute to the poem's theme, or message

To analyze how a particular stanza fits into the overall structure of a text and contributes to the development of the theme, consider the following questions:

- ✓ What poetic form does the poet use? What is the structure?

- ✓ How do the lengths of the lines and stanzas affect the meaning?

- ✓ How does a poem's stanza fit into the structure of the poem overall?

- ✓ How does the form and structure affect the poem's meaning?

- ✓ In what way does a specific stanza contribute to the poem's theme?

Skill:
Poetic Elements And Structure

Reread lines 8–18 of "I, Too, Sing America." Then, using the Checklist on the previous page, answer the multiple-choice questions below.

⟳ YOUR TURN

1. How does the stanza from lines 8–14 convey a message to the reader?

   ○ A. It suggests that what the speaker hopes for will never happen.

   ○ B. It sends the message of the hope for equality in America.

   ○ C. It implies that the speaker will continue to wait.

   ○ D. It suggests that the speaker has given up.

2. What clues tell you the poem is open form?

   ○ A. The poem has a predictable rhythm scheme.

   ○ B. The words rhyme at the end of the lines.

   ○ C. It doesn't have consistent meter, rhyme, or stanza length.

   ○ D. There is a pattern of stressed and unstressed syllables.

3. How do the lines and line breaks, when read aloud, help to convey the theme of the poem?

   ○ A. Each idea is spoken calmly, with hope, and with confidence.

   ○ B. The speaker sounds angry, rushing to express something upsetting.

   ○ C. The short lines and line breaks suggest the speaker is tired and depressed.

   ○ D. Each line seems to express a threatening demand.

Please note that excerpts and passages in the StudySync® library and this workbook are intended as touchstones to generate interest in an author's work. The excerpts and passages do not substitute for the reading of entire texts, and StudySync® strongly recommends that students seek out and purchase the whole literary or informational work in order to experience it as the author intended. Links to online resellers are available in our digital library. In addition, complete works may be ordered through an authorized reseller by filling out and returning to StudySync® the order form enclosed in this workbook.

Reading & Writing
Companion

37

Skill:
Media

Use the Checklist to analyze Media in "I, Too, Sing America." Refer to the sample student annotations about Media in the text.

••• CHECKLIST FOR MEDIA

In order to determine how to compare and contrast reading a story, drama, or poem to listening to or viewing an audio, video, or live version of a text, do the following:

- ✓ choose a story that has been presented in multiple forms of media, such as a written story and a film adaptation

- ✓ think about the key features of the different media presentations

- ✓ consider how different kinds of media treat story elements in different ways

- ✓ think about what you "see"—or visualize—as well as "hear" when you read a story, drama, or poem and how it compares to seeing it as a film, or hearing it read aloud

To compare and contrast the experience of reading a story, drama, or poem to listening to or viewing an audio, video, or live version of the text, including contrasting what they "see" and "hear" when reading the text to what they perceive when they listen or watch, consider the following questions:

- ✓ What features of each medium are the most important?

- ✓ Do you listen to it or view it? Do you hear one voice or many? How do these affect the written work?

- ✓ How is the way you picture a character in your mind as you read similar to the way that same character is portrayed in a filmed version of the same story? How is it different?

Skill:
Media

Reread lines 4–10 of "I, Too, Sing America." Then, using the Checklist on the previous page, answer the multiple-choice questions below.

⟳ YOUR TURN

1. How can comparing and contrasting different forms of media be useful for analyzing the theme of "I, Too?

   ○ A. Varying themes help the reader understand how the piece connects to the world today.
   ○ B. A shift in mood helps the reader draw further conclusions about the speaker.
   ○ C. Analyzing tone and use of pronouns helps the reader to better understand theme.
   ○ D. A shift in tone can help the reader visualize the events in the piece.

2. How are the audio and printed versions of the poem "I, Too" different?

   ○ A. The textual difference between the spoken and written version influences the audience's understanding of the poem's theme
   ○ B. The difference in the rhyming lines between the spoken and written version impacts how the reader imagines the speaker.
   ○ C. The difference in the theme between the spoken and written version allows the reader to relate to the speaker.
   ○ D. The student is better able to analyze the narrator's tone in the printed version.

Close Read

Reread "I, Too, Sing America." As you reread, complete the Skills Focus questions below. Then use your answers and annotations from the questions to help you complete the Write activity.

◎ SKILLS FOCUS

1. Explain the effect of two or three lines, or a stanza, on the poem's theme.

2. Hughes uses a dining table as a metaphor to explain American racism. Explain how this metaphor causes readers to think about the topic in a new way.

3. Compare and contrast the experience of determining the central theme of the poem by reading the poem and listening to the audio version. Explain your thinking using textual evidence.

4. Explain why it's important for the speaker to sit at the table, even though he was instructed to sit in the kitchen. Cite traits of the speaker that will help him achieve this goal.

✎ WRITE

LITERARY ANALYSIS: How does Langston Hughes use poetic elements and structure to explore the theme of change in his poem "I, Too"? Write a response in which you analyze the effect of the poem's poetic structure. Did the effect change when you listened to the poem? Be sure to use evidence from the text.

Everybody Jump

(from 'What If?')

INFORMATIONAL TEXT
Randall Munroe
2014

Introduction

Randall Munroe (b. 1984) is a physicist and former NASA computer programmer and roboticist. After leaving NASA, he became a popular webcomic artist and blogger, and in 2014, Munroe published a collection of writings and blog posts titled *What If? Serious Scientific Answers to Absurd Hypothetical Questions*. True to the collection's title, the excerpted essay explores what might happen if everyone on Earth jumped at the exact same moment. In answering this, Munroe contrasts human beings' relative unimportance in the physical universe to our profound

"At the stroke of noon, everyone jumps."

Skill: Technical Language

I think the subject of the text is "science" because the author mentions ScienceBlogs. I can guess that "kinematics" has to do with motion because everyone will jump. If the text is about motion, the type of science is probably physics.

1 *What would happen if everyone on earth stood as close to each other as they could and jumped, everyone landing on the ground at the same instant?*
   —Thomas Bennett (and many others)

2 This is one of the most popular questions submitted to this blog. It's been examined before, including by a ScienceBlogs post and a Straight Dope article. They cover the kinematics pretty well. However, they don't tell the whole story.

3 Let's take a closer look.

4 At the start of the **scenario,** the entire Earth's population has been magically transported together into one place.

5 This crowd takes up an area the size of Rhode Island. But there's no reason to use the vague phrase "an area the size of Rhode Island". This is our scenario; we can be specific. They're *actually* in Rhode Island.

6   At the stroke of noon, everyone jumps.

7   As discussed elsewhere, it doesn't really affect the planet. Earth outweighs us by a factor of over ten trillion. On average, we humans can vertically jump maybe half a meter on a good day. Even if the Earth were **rigid** and responded instantly, it would be pushed down by less than an atom's width.[1]

8   Next, everyone falls back to the ground.

Skill: Informational Text Structure

Next is one of the key signal words for sequential order, so I know to look out for other words or phrases that signal events are happening in a specific order, like "eventually" and "seconds pass" below. The sequential order helps me understand what's going to happen next in the scenario.

9   Technically, this delivers a lot of energy into the Earth, but it's spread out over a large enough area that it doesn't do much more than leave footprints in a lot of gardens. A slight pulse of pressure spreads through the North American continental crust and dissipates with little effect. The sound of all those feet hitting the ground creates a loud, drawn-out roar which lasts many seconds.

10 Eventually, the air grows quiet.

11 Seconds pass. Everyone looks around.

---

1. **atom's width:** the atom is the basic unit of matter

NOTES

12 There are a lot of uncomfortable glances. Someone coughs.

Skill: Informational Text Structure

The author is using cause-and-effect structure here to develop the story. The cause is that everybody tries to use their cell phones at the same time. The effect is that the cell networks stop working. This helps me understand the consequences of the jump.

---

13 A cell phone comes out of a pocket. Within seconds, the rest of the world's five billion phones follow. All of them—even those **compatible** with the region's towers—are displaying some version of "NO SIGNAL." The cell networks have all collapsed under the unprecedented load.

14 The T. F. Green airport in Warwick, Rhode Island handles a few thousand passengers a day. Assuming they got things organized (including sending out scouting missions to retrieve fuel), they could run at 500% **capacity** for years without making a dent in the crowd.

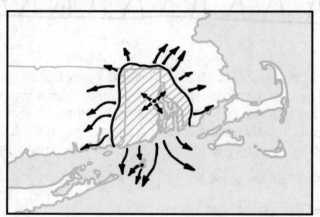

15 The addition of all the nearby airports doesn't change the equation much. Nor does the region's light rail system. Crowds climb on board container ships in the deepwater port of Providence, but stocking sufficient food and water for a long sea voyage proves a challenge.

16 Rhode Island's half-million cars are commandeered. Moments later, I-95, I-195, and I-295 become the sites of the largest traffic jam in the history of the planet. Most of the cars are engulfed by the crowds, but a lucky few get out and begin wandering the abandoned road network.

NOTES

17 Some make it past New York or Boston before running out of fuel. Since the electricity is probably not on at this point, rather than find a working gas pump, it's easier to just abandon the car and steal the new one. Who can stop you? All the cops are in Rhode Island.

18 The edge of the crowd spreads outward into southern Massachusetts and Connecticut. Any two people who meet are unlikely to have a language in common, and almost nobody knows the area. The state becomes a patchwork chaos of **coalescing** and collapsing social hierarchies.[2] Violence is common. Everybody is hungry and thirsty. Grocery stores are emptied. Fresh water is hard to come by and there's no efficient system for distributing it.

19 Within weeks, Rhode Island is a graveyard of billions.

20 The survivors spread out across the face of the world and struggle to build a new civilization atop the pristine ruins of the old. Our species staggers on, but our population has been greatly reduced. Earth's orbit is completely unaffected—it spins along exactly as it did before our species-wide jump.

21 But at least now we know.

Everybody Jump" from WHAT IF?: Serious Scientific Answers to Absurd Hypothetical Questions by Randall Munroe. Copyright © 2014 by xked Inc. Reprinted by permission of Houghton Mifflin Harcourt Publishing Company. All rights reserved.

2. **hierarchies:** structures of status or value, from the powerful to the subjugated

Please note that excerpts and passages in the StudySync® library and this workbook are intended as touchstones to generate interest in an author's work. The excerpts and passages do not substitute for the reading of entire texts, and StudySync® strongly recommends that students seek out and purchase the whole literary or informational work in order to experience it as the author intended. Links to online resellers are available in our digital library. In addition, complete works may be ordered through an authorized reseller by filling out and returning to StudySync® the order form enclosed in this workbook.

Reading & Writing Companion 45

First Read

Read the essay "Everybody Jump." After you read, complete the Think Questions below.

☁ THINK QUESTIONS

1. Why does the author of this essay choose to answer this seemingly absurd question? What is his purpose in doing so? Explain by citing textual evidence from the selection to support your answer.

2. According to the author, how would a coordinated jump affect the Earth's orbit? Describe in your own words what would happen, referring to specific details from the text.

3. Why is the outcome of this imaginary scenario surprising? Discuss how things turn out a little differently than expected. Be sure to cite examples.

4. The prefix *com-* means "together" or "in association with" something. Based on this clue and any other common affixes, what is the meaning of **compatible** as it is used in paragraph 13 of the excerpt? Write your definition here, explaining its roots and/or affixes.

5. According to paragraph 14, the T.F. Green airport "could run at 500% **capacity** for years." Based on context, what does the word *capacity* mean? Write your best definition here and explain how you figured out its meaning.

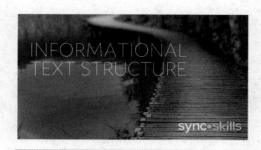

Skill:
Informational Text Structure

Use the Checklist to analyze Informational Text Structure in "Everybody Jump." Refer to the sample student annotations about Informational Text Structure in the text.

••• CHECKLIST FOR INFORMATIONAL TEXT STRUCTURE

In order to determine the overall structure of a text, note the following:

✓ the topic(s) and how the author organizes information about the topic(s)

✓ patterns in a paragraph or section of text that reveal the text structure, such as:

- sequences, including the order of events or steps in a process

- problems and their solutions

- cause-and-effect relationships

- comparisons

✓ the overall structure of the text and how each section contributes to the development of ideas

To analyze how a particular sentence, paragraph, chapter, or section fits into the overall structure of a text and contributes to the development of the ideas, use the following questions as a guide:

✓ What organizational patterns reveal the text structure the author uses to present information?

✓ How does a particular sentence, paragraph, chapter, or section fit into the overall structure of the text? How does it affect the development of the author's ideas?

✓ In what ways does the text structure contribute to the development of ideas in the text?

Please note that excerpts and passages in the StudySync® library and this workbook are intended as touchstones to generate interest in an author's work. The excerpts and passages do not substitute for the reading of entire texts, and StudySync® strongly recommends that students seek out and purchase the whole literary or informational work in order to experience it as the author intended. Links to online resellers are available in our digital library. In addition, complete works may be ordered through an authorized reseller by filling out and returning to StudySync® the order form enclosed in this workbook.

Reading & Writing Companion   47

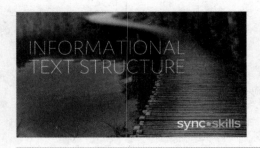

Skill:
Informational Text Structure

Reread paragraphs 14–18 of "Everybody Jump." Then, using the Checklist on the previous page, answer the multiple-choice questions below.

⟳ YOUR TURN

1. In paragraphs 14 and 15, the author uses a problem-and-solution structure. What problem are the suggested solutions trying to solve?

   ○ A. how to get people home from Rhode Island after the jump
   ○ B. how to find fuel for airplanes
   ○ C. how to direct people to the nearest train station
   ○ D. how to prepare ships for a long sea voyage

2. In paragraph 16, what text structure do the phrases "moments later" and "begin wandering" suggest?

   ○ A. classify information
   ○ B. compare and contrast
   ○ C. chronological order
   ○ D. order of important ideas

3. Which of the following descriptions in paragraph 18 is most relevant to the central idea of the text?

   ○ A. the disadvantages of knowing multiple languages
   ○ B. the effects of collapsing social hierarchies
   ○ C. the common problems when people don't know an area
   ○ D. the crowds in Massachusetts and Connecticut

Skill:
Technical Language

Use the Checklist to analyze Technical Language in "Everybody Jump." Refer to the sample student annotations about Technical Language in the text.

••• CHECKLIST FOR TECHNICAL LANGUAGE

In order to determine the meaning of words and phrases as they are used in a text, note the following:

✓ the subject of the book or article

✓ any unfamiliar words that you think might be technical terms

✓ words have multiple meanings that change when used with a specific subject

✓ the possible contextual meaning of a word, or the definition from a dictionary

To determine the meaning of words and phrases as they are used in a text, including technical meanings, consider the following questions:

✓ What is the subject of the informational text?

✓ Are there any unfamiliar words that look as if they might be technical language?

✓ Do any of the words in the text have more than one meaning?

✓ Can you identify the contextual meaning of any of the words?

Please note that excerpts and passages in the StudySync® library and this workbook are intended as touchstones to generate interest in an author's work. The excerpts and passages do not substitute for the reading of entire texts, and StudySync® strongly recommends that students seek out and purchase the whole literary or informational work in order to experience it as the author intended. Links to online resellers are available in our digital library. In addition, complete works may be ordered through an authorized reseller by filling out and returning to StudySync® the order form enclosed in this workbook.

Reading & Writing Companion 49

Skill:
Technical Language

Reread paragraphs 19–21 of "Everybody Jump." Then, using the Checklist on the previous page, answer the multiple-choice questions below.

⟳ YOUR TURN

1. Which of the following best defines "species" as it is used in the passage?

   ○ A. coined money
   ○ B. humans inhabiting the earth
   ○ C. animals of the same biological classification
   ○ D. plants of the same group

2. Which line helps you best determine the meaning of "orbit" in paragraph 20?

   ○ A. "The survivors spread out across the face of the world. . ."
   ○ B. "Our species staggers on. . ."
   ○ C. ". . . it spins along exactly as it did before our species-wide jump."
   ○ D. ". . . but our population has been greatly reduced."

Close Read

Reread "Everybody Jump." As you reread, complete the Skills Focus questions below. Then use your answers and annotations from the questions to help you complete the Write activity.

◎ SKILLS FOCUS

1. Identify examples of the author's use of a cause-and-effect text structure. Explain what details or signal words reveal the text structure.

2. Identify a place in the text where the author uses another text structure that helps develop the central idea of the text. Explain what details or signal words reveal the text structure.

3. Identify a technical meaning of a word in the text and the context clues you used to help you define it.

4. Think about the unit's essential question: How do you know what to do when there are no instructions? Identify textual evidence in Munroe's scenario that answers this question, and explain your reasoning.

✏ WRITE

NARRATIVE: Randall Munroe describes the effect of everyone on Earth jumping at the same time as they stand close together. Imagine that you are one of these jumping individuals. Write a scene describing the incident from your point of view. What do you see? How do you **maneuver** yourself and others through the chaos? Draw inspiration for your narrative using evidence from the various informational text structures in Munroe's essay as you write your narrative.

Please note that excerpts and passages in the StudySync® library and this workbook are intended as touchstones to generate interest in an author's work. The excerpts and passages do not substitute for the reading of entire texts, and StudySync® strongly recommends that students seek out and purchase the whole literary or informational work in order to experience it as the author intended. Links to online resellers are available in our digital library. In addition, complete works may be ordered through an authorized reseller by filling out and returning to StudySync® the order form enclosed in this workbook.

Reading & Writing Companion   51

Hoot

FICTION
Carl Hiaasen
2002

Introduction

After a move from Montana to Florida, Roy is the new kid in town, with no friends and no allies—not yet, anyway. One day, with his face smashed against the school bus window courtesy of the school bully, Roy sees something that attracts his curiosity. This coming-of-age novel, written by Carl Hiaasen (b. 1953) was awarded a Newbery Honor in 2003.

"... Roy lowered the window and stuck out his head. The strange boy was gone."

1 Excerpted from Chapter 1

2 Roy would not have noticed the strange boy if it weren't for Dana Matherson, because Roy ordinarily didn't look out the window of the school bus. He preferred to read comics and mystery books on the morning ride to Trace Middle.

3 But on this day, a Monday (Roy would never forget), Dana Matherson grabbed Roy's head from behind and pressed his thumbs into Roy's temple, as if he were squeezing a soccer ball. The older kids were supposed to stay in the back of the bus, but Dana had snuck up behind Roy's seat and **ambushed** him. When Roy tried to wriggle free, Dana mushed his face against the window.

4 It was then, squinting through the smudged glass, that Roy spotted the strange boy running along the sidewalk. It appeared as if he was hurrying to catch the school bus, which had stopped at a corner to pick up more kids.

5 The boy was straw-blond and wiry, and his skin was nutbrown from the sun. The **expression** on his face was **intent** and serious. He wore a faded Miami Heat basketball jersey and dirty khaki shorts, and here was the odd part: no shoes. The soles of his bare feet looked as black as barbecue coals.

6 Trace Middle School didn't have the world's strictest dress code, but Roy was pretty sure that some sort of footwear was **required**. The boy might have been carrying sneakers in his backpack, if only he'd been wearing a backpack. No shoes, no backpack, no books—strange, indeed, on a school day.

7 Roy was sure that the barefoot boy would catch all kinds of grief from Dana and the other big kids once he boarded the bus, but that didn't happen. . . .

8 Because the boy kept running—past the corner, past the line of students waiting to get on the bus; past the bus itself. Roy wanted to shout, "Hey, look at that guy!" but his mouth wasn't working so well. Dana Matherson still had him from behind, pushing his face against the window.

Skill:
Theme

One detail I notice is that Roy is getting bullied. When I read how Roy reacts to Dana's bullying, I can infer a theme. Roy's curiosity about the running boy makes him immune to his pain. Maybe one way to escape bullying is to check out mentally.

9 As the bus pulled away from the intersection, Roy hoped to catch another glimpse of the boy farther up the street. However, he had turned off the sidewalk and was now cutting across a private yard—running very fast, much faster than Roy could run and maybe even faster than Richard, Roy's best friend back in Montana. Richard was so fast that he got to work out with the high school track squad when he was only in seventh grade.

10 Dana Matherson was digging his fingernails into Roy's scalp, trying to make him squeal, but Roy barely felt a thing. He was gripped with curiosity as the running boy dashed through one neat green yard after another, getting smaller in Roy's vision as he put a wider distance between himself and the school bus.

11 Roy saw a big pointy-eared dog, probably a German shepherd, **bound** off somebody's porch and go for the boy. Incredibly, the boy didn't change his course. He vaulted over the dog, crashed through a cherry hedge, and then disappeared from view.

12 Roy gasped.

13 "Whassamatter, cowgirl? Had enough?"

14 This was Dana, hissing in Roy's right ear. Being the new kid on the bus, Roy didn't expect any help from the others. The "cowgirl" remark was so lame, it wasn't worth getting mad about. Dana was a well-known idiot, on top of which he outweighed Roy by at least fifty pounds. Fighting back would have been a complete waste of energy.

15 "Had enough yet? We can't hear you, Tex." Dana's breath smelled like stale cigarettes. Smoking and beating up smaller kids were his two main hobbies.

16 "Yeah, okay," Roy said impatiently. "I've had enough."

17 As soon as he was freed, Roy lowered the window and stuck out his head. The strange boy was gone.

18 Who was he? What was he running from?

19 Roy wondered if any of the other kids on the bus had seen what he'd seen. For a moment he wondered if he'd really seen it himself.

Excerpted from *Hoot* by Carl Hiaasen, published by Alfred A. Knopf.

First Read

Read *Hoot*. After you read, complete the Think Questions below.

THINK QUESTIONS

1. Why is Roy looking out the window? Cite textual evidence from the selection to support your answer.

2. Based on paragraph 4, what inferences can you make about the mysterious boy? What clues does the text give?

3. Describe the relationship between Dana and Roy, using specific examples from the text.

4. Find the word **required** in paragraph 5 of *Hoot*. Use context clues in the surrounding sentences, as well as the sentence in which the word appears, to determine the word's meaning.

5. Use context clues to determine the meaning of **bound** as it is used in paragraph 10 of *Hoot*. Write your definition here and identify clues that helped you figure out its meaning. Then check the meaning in the dictionary.

Please note that excerpts and passages in the StudySync® library and this workbook are intended as touchstones to generate interest in an author's work. The excerpts and passages do not substitute for the reading of entire texts, and StudySync® strongly recommends that students seek out and purchase the whole literary or informational work in order to experience it as the author intended. Links to online resellers are available in our digital library. In addition, complete works may be ordered through an authorized reseller by filling out and returning to StudySync® the order form enclosed in this workbook.

Reading & Writing Companion

55

Skill:
Theme

Use the Checklist to analyze Theme in *Hoot*. Refer to the sample student annotations about Theme in the text.

••• CHECKLIST FOR THEME

In order to identify a theme or central idea in a text, note the following:

✓ the topic of the text

✓ whether or not the theme is stated directly in the text

✓ details in the text that may reveal the theme

- the title and chapter headings

- details about the setting

- a narrator's or speaker's tone

- characters' thoughts, actions, and dialogue

- the central conflict in the story's plot

- the resolution of the conflict

✓ analyze how characters and the problems they face are affected by the setting, and what impact this may have on how the theme is developed

To determine a theme or central idea of a text and how it is conveyed through particular details, consider the following questions:

✓ What is a theme or central idea of the text?

✓ What details helped to reveal that theme or central idea?

✓ When did you become aware of that theme? For instance, did the story's conclusion reveal the theme?

Skill:
Theme

Reread paragraphs 14–18 from *Hoot*. Then, using the Checklist on the previous page, answer the multiple-choice questions below.

↻ YOUR TURN

1. This question has two parts. First, answer Part A. Then, answer Part B.

    Part A: In paragraph 15, how does Roy end the conflict with Dana?

    ○ A. Roy insults Dana's smoking habit, escalating the situation.
    ○ B. Roy gives in, allowing Dana to maintain the upper hand.
    ○ C. Roy begs the smaller kids on the bus for help, causing Dana to laugh.
    ○ D. Roy tells Dana not to call him "Tex," causing Dana to grab Roy's head.

    Part B: What theme can be inferred from the way Roy ends the conflict with Dana in paragraph 15?

    ○ A. During a conflict, it's best to stand up for yourself and fight back.
    ○ B. During a conflict, it's best to call someone names and invade his personal space.
    ○ C. During a conflict, it's best to stay calm and rational.
    ○ D. During a conflict, it's best to taunt and make physical attacks.

2. Throughout the story, Roy's reaction to Dana Matherson supports a theme that illustrates the value of –

    ○ A. bullying
    ○ B. curiosity
    ○ C. cleverness
    ○ D. running

Close Read

Reread *Hoot*. As you reread, complete the Skills Focus questions below. Then use your answers and annotations from the questions to help you complete the Write activity.

◎ SKILLS FOCUS

1. Dealing with Dana's bullying is one of the challenges Roy faces in the story. Identify evidence of how Roy responds to this challenge. Explain what the response helps you infer about a theme in the story.

2. Dana's bullying is not the only plot event in the chapter. Identify evidence about the other event the author **describes** and about Roy's reaction to it. Explain how the two plot events are related and how this helps you infer a second theme.

3. The author uses Roy's thoughts and actions to develop the plot. Identify examples of Roy's responses that help you understand his character. Explain how these responses help develop the plot.

4. Roy is new to Trace Middle School, so he is on his own in figuring out how to handle Dana's bullying. Identify textual evidence that highlights Roy's methods. Explain what the evidence tells you about Roy's character and the author's message.

✎ WRITE

LITERARY ANALYSIS: In *Hoot*, Roy responds to bullying in a surprising way. How does the author use details and Roy's response to Dana's bullying to communicate a theme? Do you agree or disagree with the author's message in this story? Use evidence from the text as well as from your own experiences to support your response.

Donna O'Meara: The Volcano Lady

INFORMATIONAL TEXT
McGraw Hill Education
2017

Introduction

Donna O'Meara is an explorer and adventurer like few others. As a photographer of some of the world's biggest volcanoes, her job is often quite perilous. In the face of danger, however, O'Meara often risks her life to obtain some of the most amazing up-close footage of volcanoes the world has ever witnessed. This short biography profiles O'Meara's life, from her time growing up in New England to how she came to be known as the "volcano lady."

"They were stuck on a narrow ledge just 200 feet above a fiery, smoking pit."

1   After a blistering hot day, a cold storm suddenly whipped the top of Mt. Stromboli, a volcano on an island off the coast of Sicily. The temperature quickly dropped more than 60 degrees. Donna O'Meara and her husband, Steve, didn't dare try to climb down the steep slopes in the dark. They were stuck on a narrow ledge just 200 feet above a fiery, smoking pit.

2   They huddled together, shivering nonstop in the cold air. Thundering blasts from the volcano and falling rocks the size of basketballs kept them awake and fearful. When the sun came up, Donna felt cinder burns on her face. There were sharp pieces of rock tangled in her hair.

3   Frightening experiences on top of a volcano are not unusual for Donna O'Meara. For over 25 years, she has worked with Steve to photograph and study volcanoes all over the world. They hope their documentation will someday be a written and visual record of information that helps scientists to better **predict** volcanic **eruptions.**

4   O'Meara grew up in the New England countryside. There are no volcanoes in Connecticut, but in the spring and summer there were fierce thunder and lightning storms that thrilled Donna. In school, her favorite classes were earth science and biology. However, instead of turning her love for science into a career after graduation, she became an artist, photographer, and writer. As she worked on different magazines and books, she gradually began to realize that something was missing in her life.

5   When Donna went back to school at the age of 32 to study science, her passion for volcanoes began. She took geology classes to learn more about what rocks and soil tell us about the earth. She found out that volcanism is one of the most **dynamic** forces in nature. Volcanoes constantly shape and change the earth. Many islands, such as the islands that make up Hawaii, were formed by volcanic activity.

6   In 1986, Donna visited her first volcano as Steve's research assistant. After dodging lava bombs and feeling the heat from underground lava melting her shoes, Donna was hooked. The following year, she and Steve were married

Copyright © BookheadEd Learning, LLC

on lava that had oozed from Kilauea on Hawaii and hardened. Lava that hardens creates new landforms, and some volcanoes, such as Surtsey off the coast of Iceland, actually create new islands!

7   Today, Donna can't imagine what her life would be like without volcanoes. She loves them so much she lives on one. Her home is on top of Kilauea, where she was married. This is one of the most **active** volcanoes in the world.

Kilauea, in Hawaii

8   From their home, Donna and Steve run Volcano Watch International (VWI). The O'Mearas' organization is dedicated to understanding how Earth's active volcanoes work. VWI uses photos and video to educate people about the dangers of volcanoes. Their mission is to travel to active volcanoes and **document** the eruptions. The first volcano Donna studied was Kilauea, which is a shield volcano.

9   Mt. Stromboli is a stratovolcano. A stratovolcano has the common cone shape people usually picture when they think of a volcano. It is formed from explosive eruptions that build layers of ash, lava, and cinders at the top of the mountain.

10   Donna says the experience of being stranded on Mt. Stromboli for one freezing night was the scariest experience of her life. Since the sides of this volcano are steep, it was impossible for the O'Mearas to travel down the slopes until the sun rose in the morning. So they were trapped on a ledge in the freezing cold with scalding rocks flying around them.

11   Donna O'Meara escaped from her scary night of Mt. Stromboli safe and sound. Now she and Steve hope that the knowledge they gather photographing and studying volcanoes will help save the lives of people who live near them. The O'Mearas' volcano photographs, videos, and samples of volcanic rock are part of the permanent collection of the Smithsonian Institution located in Washington, D.C.

12   Donna believes they have the best jobs on Earth, even though their work may be the most dangerous as well.

Used with permission of McGraw-Hill Education

Please note that excerpts and passages in the StudySync® library and this workbook are intended as touchstones to generate interest in an author's work. The excerpts and passages do not substitute for the reading of entire texts, and StudySync® strongly recommends that students seek out and purchase the whole literary or informational work in order to experience it as the author intended. Links to online resellers are available in our digital library. In addition, complete works may be ordered through an authorized reseller by filling out and returning to StudySync® the order form enclosed in this workbook.

Reading & Writing Companion   **61**

WRITE

PERSONAL RESPONSE: Donna O'Meara and her husband Steve risk their lives to collect close-up photos of volcanoes from around the world. If you were a scientist or researcher, what kind of natural phenomenon would you want to explore? Why? Support your response with evidence from the text and from your personal experience. As you make connections between Donna O'Meara's dream and your own, include any information that may have changed your understanding or opinion of what it means to be a scientist or researcher.

Dare To Be Creative!

INFORMATIONAL TEXT
Madeleine L'Engle
1983

Introduction

n 1983, renowned young adult author Madeleine L'Engle (1918–2007) delivered this lecture before the Library of Congress. "Dare to be creative!" is heralded as an inspirational manifesto on the beauty and power of words, the magic of reading, as well as a stunning rebuke of literary censorship. L'Engle is the author of such young adult classics as *A Wrinkle in Time* and *A Wind in the Door*.

"My books push me and prod me and make me ask questions I might otherwise avoid."

1   We need to dare disturb the universe by not being **manipulated** or frightened by judgmental groups who assume the right to insist that if we do not agree with them, not only do we not understand but we are wrong. How dull the world would be if we all had to feel the same way about everything, if we all had to like the same books, dislike the same books. For my relaxing reading I enjoy English murder mysteries, but my husband prefers spy thrillers. I like beet greens and he likes beet root. We would be a society of ants if we couldn't have personal tastes and honest differences. And how sad it would be if we had to give up all sense of mystery for the limited world of provable fact. I still can't read *The Happy Prince* or *The Selfish Giant* aloud without a lump coming into my throat, but I suppose that talking statues and giants are on someone's hit list.

2   Perhaps some of this zeal is caused by fear. But, as Bertrand Russell warns, "Zeal is a bad mark for a cause. Nobody had any zeal about arithmetic. It was the anti-vaccinationists,[1] not the vaccinationists, who were **zealous.**" Yet because those who were not threatened by the idea of vaccination ultimately won out, we have **eradicated** the horror of smallpox[2] from the planet.

3   It is hard for us to understand the zeal of the medical **establishment** when Dr. Semmelweis sensibly suggested that it might be a good idea if surgeons washed their hands after dissecting a cadaver, before going to deliver a woman in labor. This, to us, obvious suggestions of cleanliness was so threatening to the medical establishment of the day that they zealously set about persecuting

Despite overzealous critics, Dr. Semmelweis convinced doctors to wash their hands when dealing with patients, which saved many lives.

---

1. **anti-vaccinationists:** activists or individuals who oppose the practice of giving vaccinations or shots
2. **smallpox:** a lethal and disfiguring infectious virus eradicated in 1980

Semmelweis. But, thanks to him, many of us are alive because doctors now wash their hands. If the zealots had won, women would still be dying of septicemia[3] after childbirth.

4   Russell suggests that people are zealous when they are not completely certain they are right. I agree with him. When I find myself hotly defending something, when I am, in fact, zealous, it is time for me to step back and examine whatever it is that has me so hot under the collar. Do I think it's going to threaten my comfortable **rut?** Make me change and grow?—and growing always causes growing pains. Am I afraid to ask questions?

5   Sometimes. But I believe that good questions are more important than answers, and the best children's books ask questions, and make the reader ask questions. And every new question is going to disturb someone's universe.

6   Writing fiction is definitely a universe disturber, and for the writer, first of all. My books push me and prod me and make me ask questions I might otherwise avoid. I start a book, having lived with the characters for several years, during the writing of other books, and I have a pretty good idea of where the story is going and what I hope it's going to say. And then, once I get deep into the writing, unexpected things begin to happen, things which make me question, and which sometimes really shake my universe.

By Madeleine L'Engle, 1983. Used by permission of Crosswicks Ltd., c/o Aaron M. Priest Literary Agency

---

3. **septicemia:** a bacterial infection of the blood, skin or lungs

✏ WRITE

PERSONAL RESPONSE: In the speech "Dare to be Creative!," Madeleine L'Engle urges listeners to not be scared of thinking independently. Write about a time when you took a risk to do something creative or unexpected and it turned out well. Then, explain how this connects to the speech. Support your response with evidence from the text as well as personal experience.

Please note that excerpts and passages in the StudySync® library and this workbook are intended as touchstones to generate interest in an author's work. The excerpts and passages do not substitute for the reading of entire texts, and StudySync® strongly recommends that students seek out and purchase the whole literary or informational work in order to experience it as the author intended. Links to online resellers are available in our digital library. In addition, complete works may be ordered through an authorized reseller by filling out and returning to StudySync® the order form enclosed in this workbook.

Reading & Writing Companion   **65**

Margaret Bourke-White:
Fearless Photographer

INFORMATIONAL TEXT
McGraw Hill Education
2017

Introduction

Margaret Bourke-White (1904–1971) was an American photographer who gained fame for traveling around the world and snapping photographs for high-profile magazines. As the first American female war photojournalist, her photographs earned her a spot on the cover of *Life* magazine and can be viewed to this day in museums nationwide, including the Library of Congress. This short biography of her life describes some of the challenges she faced and feats she accomplished throughout her career.

". . . Margaret made the production of steel look magnificent, mysterious, and awe-inspiring."

1   In 1904, girls weren't supposed to dream of careers that took them flying into the sky on airplanes or climbing out onto ledges at the top of skyscrapers. And they certainly weren't encouraged to think about competing with men for the opportunity to photograph important people and events.

2   Joseph White and Minnie Bourke, however, never told their daughter what to think and dream about. Instead, young Margaret, or "Peg" as her friends called her, got plenty of attention and encouragement from her parents to explore her world. Early on, they taught her to work hard and to go after what she wanted. They even gave her a motto: "You can." It's no wonder Margaret Bourke-White grew up to be one of the most accomplished women and talked-about photographers of the twentieth century.

Margaret Bourke-White paved the way for female photographers.

3   Many photographers today owe thanks to Margaret. From the time she started taking photographs and recognized that they could stir up feelings to the **culmination** of her long career as a photojournalist, Margaret was a trailblazer.[1] She shaped the art of photography and the profession of photojournalism and showed that women photographers could travel all over the world and work alongside men in dangerous situations.

4   **A Star Photographer**

5   Her mother gave Margaret her first camera in 1921, when she was 17 years old. Her interest in photography grew as a result of her father's enthusiasm for cameras. A few years later, Margaret's classmates at Cornell University became her first admirers when photos she took of the campus appeared in

**Skill:
Textual Evidence**

I can find evidence explicitly in the text that supports the idea that Margaret was a trailblazer. I highlighted the "firsts" in her career.

Skill: Technical Language

I'm not sure what a "commercial photography studio" is, but the text says that Margaret opened one, so it's probably a business.

---

1. **trailblazer:** someone who does things for the first time, metaphorically burning a trail for others

 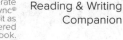

Skill:
Textual Evidence

Margaret Bourke-White was a great photographer, but she did more than just take photographs. The text doesn't explicitly say that she was an inventor because this sentence has an implicit meaning. I made an inference to figure it out.

the school newspapers. A year after graduating, Margaret moved to Cleveland, Ohio and opened a commercial photography studio.

6   One of Margaret's first clients was the Otis Steel Company. Her success was due both to her technique and her skills in dealing with people. At first, several people at the company wondered if a woman could stand up to the intense heat and generally dirty and gritty conditions inside a steel mill.[2] When Margaret finally got permission, the technical problems began. Black-and-white film at that time was sensitive to blue light, not the reds and oranges of hot steel. The pictures came out all black. Margaret solved this problem by bringing along a new style of flare (which produces white light) and having assistants hold them to light her scenes. Her abilities resulted in some of the best steel factory pictures of that era, and these earned her national attention.

7   The city's powerful businessmen soon began calling on her to take pictures of their mills, factories, and buildings. In the steel mills, she wanted to be right next to the melted metal. The extreme heat sometimes burned her face and damaged the paint on her camera. In her first well-known photographs, Margaret made the production of steel look magnificent, mysterious, and awe-inspiring. Her photos, filled with streams of melted steel and flying sparks, caught the eye of someone who would change her life.

8   **A New Sort of Storytelling**

9   Henry Luce was a powerful and important American publisher. In the 1920s and 1930s he started a series of magazines that would change journalism and the reading habits of Americans. Luce's magazine called *Time* summarized and **interpreted** the week's news. *Life* was a picture magazine of politics, culture and society that became very popular in the years before television, and *Fortune* explored the economy and the world of business. *Sports Illustrated* investigated the teams and important players of popular sports such as baseball and football.

10 In 1929, Henry Luce invited Margaret to work at *Fortune* Magazine. She jumped at the chance and became the first woman in a new field called photojournalism, in which photographers reported the news through images.

11 As Margaret snapped artistic shots of workplaces, she was able to find beauty in simple objects. Over time she **adapted** her techniques to photograph people and was **adept** at catching expressions and showing hardship. In 1930, she was the first photographer from a Western country to be allowed

2. **steel mill:** a plant where part or all of the steelmaking process is done

into the Soviet Union (now Russia), where she took pictures of the workers in what was then a communist[3] country.

12 **World War II and After**

13 When World War II broke out in 1939, Margaret became the first female war correspondent. This is a journalist who covers stories first hand from a war zone. In 1941, she traveled to the Soviet Union again and was the only foreign photographer in Moscow when German forces invaded. Taking shelter in the U.S. Embassy,[4] she then captured much of the fierce battle on camera.

14 As the war continued, Margaret joined the U.S. Army Air Force in North Africa and then traveled with the U.S. Army in Italy and later Germany. She repeatedly came under fire in Italy as she traveled through areas of intense fighting.

15 After the war, Margaret continued to make the world's most complex events understandable. Her photos reflected stirring social issues of the time. She photographed South Africans laboring in gold mines and civil rights leader Mahatma Gandhi's nonviolent work in India.

16 **A Lasting Influence**

17 During the 1930s and 1940s, Margaret's adventurous attitude and perseverance paved the way for women to take on roles beyond the **norm**. Rather than snapping photos of high-society parties as other female photographers had done before her, she marched into steel plants and combat zones. She proved to women that they had every right to pursue the careers they wanted.

18 Through her work, Margaret became a role model for working women as well as a strong voice for the poor and powerless. She earned the respect of powerful businessmen when women were discouraged from working. When she died in 1971, she left behind not only an amazing photographic record of the human experience. She also left a message for women all over the world who wanted to make an impact: "You can."

Used with permission by McGraw Hill Education.

> **Skill:**
> **Theme**
>
> *I know the word "technique" can have many different meanings, like having a certain technique for cooking or skateboarding! I can use the subject of the text to understand that the word "technique" here means Margaret's skills in photography.*

3. **communist:** a system of government which aims to eliminate class hierarchies by placing the means of production in common ownership
4. **U.S. Embassy:** the office of the United States in any other country

First Read

Read "Margaret Bourke-White: Fearless Photographer." After you read, complete the Think Questions below.

 THINK QUESTIONS

1. Describe one example of when Margaret Bourke-White's hardworking attitude helped advance her career. Refer to specific passages or quotations from the text in your answer.

2. What was special about how Margaret Bourke-White photographed steel mills? Use evidence from the text in your response.

3. What made Margaret Bourke-White different from other photojournalists of her time? Identify several ways in which Margaret stood out from the crowd, citing textual evidence.

4. Which context clues helped you determine the meaning of the word **adapted** in paragraph 9? Write your definition of *adapted* and describe which words in the paragraph led you to your understanding of the word. Then look up the word in a print or online dictionary to confirm your definition.

5. The word **norm** is derived from the Latin *norma*, meaning "precept" or "rule." Knowing this, try to infer the meaning of *norm* as it is used in paragraph 13. Write your best definition here, along with any other words you know that could be derived from the same Latin root.

Skill:
Textual Evidence

Use the Checklist to analyze Textual Evidence in "Margaret Bourke-White: Fearless Photographer." Refer to the sample student annotations about Textual Evidence in the text.

⟳ CHECKLIST FOR TEXTUAL EVIDENCE

In order to support an analysis by citing textual evidence that is explicitly stated in the text, do the following:

- ✓ read the text closely and critically

- ✓ identify what the text says explicitly

- ✓ find the most relevant textual evidence that supports your analysis

- ✓ consider why the author explicitly states specific details and information

- ✓ cite the specific words, phrases, sentences, or paragraphs from the text that support your analysis

In order to interpret implicit meanings in a text by making inferences, do the following:

- ✓ combine information directly stated in the text with your own knowledge, experiences, and observations

- ✓ cite the specific words, phrases, sentences, or paragraphs from the text that support this inference

In order to cite textual evidence to support an analysis of what the text says explicitly as well as inferences drawn from the text, consider the following questions:

- ✓ Have I read the text closely and critically?

- ✓ What inferences am I making about the text? What textual evidence am I using to support these inferences?

- ✓ Am I quoting the evidence from the text correctly?

- ✓ Does my textual evidence logically relate to my analysis?

Skill:
Textual Evidence

Reread paragraphs 13–14 of "Margaret Bourke-White: Fearless Photographer." Then, using the Checklist on the previous page, answer the multiple-choice questions below.

YOUR TURN

1. Using the textual evidence in paragraph 13, what is most likely an inference you can make about Margaret Bourke-White?

    ○ A. She was unable to become an advocate for women because of her profession.

    ○ B. She was able to become successful because her father was a powerful businessman.

    ○ C. She encouraged other women to pursue photography as a way to support equal rights.

    ○ D. She was an innovator and a symbol for women's rights and equality.

2. Which textual evidence best supports the author's claim in paragraph 14 that Margaret Bourke-White was "a strong voice for the poor and powerless"?

    ○ A. "Margaret's classmates at Cornell University became her first admirers when photographs she took of the campus appeared in the school newspapers."

    ○ B. "The city's powerful businessmen soon began calling on her to take pictures of their mills, factories, and buildings."

    ○ C. "As Margaret snapped artistic shots of workplaces, she was able to find beauty in simple objects."

    ○ D. "She photographed South Africans laboring in gold mines and civil rights leader Mahatma Gandhi's nonviolent work in India."

Skill:
Technical Language

Use the Checklist to analyze Technical Language in "Margaret Bourke-White: Fearless Photographer." Refer to the sample student annotations about Technical Language in the text.

⟳ CHECKLIST FOR TECHNICAL LANGUAGE

In order to determine the meaning of words and phrases as they are used in a text, note the following:

- ✓ the subject of the book or article

- ✓ any unfamiliar words that you think might be technical terms

- ✓ words have multiple meanings that change when used with a specific subject

- ✓ the possible contextual meaning of a word, or the definition from a dictionary

To determine the meaning of words and phrases as they are used in a text, including technical meanings, consider the following questions:

- ✓ What is the subject of the informational text?

- ✓ Are there any unfamiliar words that look as if they might be technical language?

- ✓ Do any of the words in the text have more than one meaning?

- ✓ Can you identify the contextual meaning of any of the words?

Please note that excerpts and passages in the StudySync® library and this workbook are intended as touchstones to generate interest in an author's work. The excerpts and passages do not substitute for the reading of entire texts, and StudySync® strongly recommends that students seek out and purchase the whole literary or informational work in order to experience it as the author intended. Links to online resellers are available in our digital library. In addition, complete works may be ordered through an authorized reseller by filling out and returning to StudySync® the order form enclosed in this workbook.

Reading & Writing Companion   **73**

Skill:
Technical Language

Reread paragraph 5 of "Margaret Bourke-White: Fearless Photographer." Then, using the Checklist on the previous page, answer the multiple-choice questions below.

↻ YOUR TURN

1. Which of the following context clues in the text help you to define the technical term "flare"?

   ○ A. "produces white light"
   ○ B. "came out all black"
   ○ C. "light her scenes"
   ○ D. "national attention"

2. Which of the following best defines "scenes" as it's used in the passage?

   ○ A. a type of camera
   ○ B. the subjects/locations of her photographs
   ○ C. a theater production
   ○ D. the film used

Close Read

Reread "Margaret Bourke-White: Fearless Photographer." As you reread, complete the Skills Focus questions below. Then use your answers and annotations from the questions to help you complete the Write activity.

◎ SKILLS FOCUS

1. "Margaret Bourke-White: Fearless Photographer" claims that Bourke-White "became a role model for working women." Identify textual evidence that supports this claim. Explain your reasoning.

2. Identify technical terms in "Margaret Bourke-White: Fearless Photographer" that relate to the subject of photography. Cite the evidence that helped you identify the terms' meanings.

3. In "Donna O'Meara: The Volcano Lady," the author presents textual evidence that suggests that O'Meara is attracted to the adventure of photographing volcanoes. Identify evidence in "Margaret Bourke-White: Fearless Photographer" that suggests that Bourke-White was also motivated by a sense of adventure. Use the evidence to compare and contrast the career motivations of the two women.

4. "Margaret Bourke-White: Fearless Photographer" calls Bourke-White a trailblazer. Identify textual evidence that supports this claim. Explain how the evidence relates to the unit's essential question: How do you know what to do when there are no instructions?

✏ WRITE

COMPARATIVE: "Donna O'Meara: The Volcano Lady," "'Dare to Be Creative!," and "Margaret Bourke-White: Fearless Photographer" each describe a person motivated to do something other people see as impossible. They refuse to be manipulated into one way of thinking or living. Some people are motivated by role models or successes, while other people derive motivation from their experiences. Compare and contrast the main motivation of each individual in these three texts, using technical language when possible. Remember to use evidence from all three texts to support your ideas.

Please note that excerpts and passages in the StudySync® library and this workbook are intended as touchstones to generate interest in an author's work. The excerpts and passages do not substitute for the reading of entire texts, and StudySync® strongly recommends that students seek out and purchase the whole literary or informational work in order to experience it as the author intended. Links to online resellers are available in our digital library. In addition, complete works may be ordered through an authorized reseller by filling out and returning to StudySync® the order form enclosed in this workbook.

Reading & Writing Companion   **75**

Extended Writing Project

Informative Writing Process: Plan

| PLAN | DRAFT | REVISE | EDIT AND PUBLISH |

The texts in this unit feature individuals who are driven to act without instructions, a clear plan, or a certain outcome. Margaret Bourke-White became the first female war photojournalist, sacrificing her safety in order to capture important moments in history. In one of the most popular Greek myths, Perseus sets out on a quest to defeat the snake-haired Gorgon, Medusa. He does not know if he'll survive the battle. Hatshepsut became the first female leader in ancient Egypt to call herself "pharaoh," breaking tradition and gender barriers throughout her reign. What motivates, or moves, these individuals to attempt something no one has done before?

WRITING PROMPT

What motivates us to conquer feelings of uncertainty?

Think about the individuals from this unit who take action even when they are unsure of what lies ahead. Identify three of these individuals and write an informative essay explaining what drives them to respond, take action, or make a decision when there are no guidelines to help them. Be sure your informative essay includes the following:

- an introduction
- a thesis or controlling idea
- coherent body paragraphs
- supporting details
- a conclusion

Writing to Sources

As you gather ideas and information from the texts in the unit, be sure to:

- use evidence from multiple sources; and
- avoid overly relying on one source.

Please note that excerpts and passages in the StudySync® library and this workbook are intended as touchstones to generate interest in an author's work. The excerpts and passages do not substitute for the reading of entire texts, and StudySync® strongly recommends that students seek out and purchase the whole literary or informational work in order to experience it as the author intended. Links to online resellers are available in our digital library. In addition, complete works may be ordered through an authorized reseller by filling out and returning to StudySync® the order form enclosed in this workbook.

Reading & Writing Companion 77

Introduction to Informative Writing

Writers of informative texts provide facts and details related to historical, scientific, and cultural topics. An informative text presents readers with information, facts, and ideas about real people, places, things, and events. The text should include an introduction with a thesis statement, or the main idea about the topic, body paragraphs that include details that support the main idea, and a conclusion.

Text structure refers to the way a writer organizes the information in a nonfiction text. It is an organizational pattern that is used to present facts and other information clearly. There are several different types of informative text structures. For instance, a writer may:

- describe a process or a series of steps to follow in sequential order
- tell about events in chronological order
- discuss ideas in order of importance
- compare and contrast information
- present cause and effect relationships
- list advantages and disadvantages
- describe a problem and offer a solution
- define the essential, or most important, qualities of a subject
- classify, or organize, information into categories and subcategories

A writer may use more than one organizational pattern within the same text. In addition, a text structure can be used to organize information about more than one topic.

Analyzing the structure of an informative text helps a reader to follow what a writer is trying to say and understand how different facts and details are related. It can also help a reader identify the main, or controlling, idea.

As you continue with this Extended Writing Project, you'll receive more instruction and practice at crafting each of the characteristics of informative writing. This will help you to create your own informative text.

Before you get started on your own informative text, read this informative essay that one student, Colin, wrote in response to the writing prompt. As you read the Model, highlight and annotate the features of informative writing that Colin included in his text.

≡ STUDENT MODEL

1   Sometimes people are motivated to take action without really knowing why. It could be a feeling, a goal, or a person that encourages them. Scientist Donna O'Meara is motivated by a desire to understand something dangerous. She also wants to help others. The character Roy in Carl Hiaasen's book *Hoot* is motivated by curiosity. His quick-witted thinking helps him out. Author Randall Munroe is motivated by mathematical reasoning. He wants to answer what seems to be an impossible question. Each of these people or characters has a different motivation and faces different obstacles and problems, but they all learn something important.

2   Donna O'Meara's desire to understand how volcanoes work has sometimes put her in danger. Most people would probably be afraid to get close to a volcano. There's a lot we don't know about them. But O'Meara has risked her life to study them. During her first visit to a volcano, she dodged "lava bombs," and hot lava melted her shoes. Another time, she and her husband Steve "were trapped on a ledge in the freezing cold with scalding rocks flying around them." The desire for knowledge has pushed O'Meara to conquer the unknown and hazardous world of volcanoes. Now she's an expert on volcanoes. She shares her knowledge to help keep others safe when volcanoes erupt. She hopes her work will "help save the lives of people who live near" volcanoes.

3   Like Donna O'Meara, the character Roy in *Hoot* is motivated by a desire for knowledge. He's also clever when it comes to dealing with problems. These qualities help Roy, who's the new kid at school, deal with Dana the bully. Dana is attacking Roy on his way to school when Roy sees a boy running past the school bus. Even though Dana is hurting him, Roy is "gripped with curiosity" about the boy: "Who was he? What was he running from?" Roy doesn't care about the pain. He just wants Dana to stop bothering him, and he is smarter than Dana. Although Roy might not know the boy running past the

Please note that excerpts and passages in the StudySync® library and this workbook are intended as touchstones to generate interest in an author's work. The excerpts and passages do not substitute for the reading of entire texts, and StudySync® strongly recommends that students seek out and purchase the whole literary or informational work in order to experience it as the author intended. Links to online resellers are available in our digital library. In addition, complete works may be ordered through an authorized reseller by filling out and returning to StudySync® the order form enclosed in this workbook.

Reading & Writing
Companion

79

NOTES

bus, he does know that Dana is "a well-known idiot." Roy also knows that fighting back would be "a complete waste of energy." When Roy tells Dana "I've had enough," Dana lets him go. Now Roy, released from the grip of Dana's hands, is free to wonder about the strange boy. Roy's curiosity and his intelligence help him get out of a bad situation.

4   In "Everybody Jump," scientist Randall Munroe is motivated to use mathematical reasoning to answer a difficult question: "What would happen if everyone on earth stood as close to each other as they could and jumped . . . at the same instant?" This could never happen in real life, but Munroe takes the question seriously. He knows that "many others" are curious about this topic and uncertain about the answer. Munroe uses mathematical reasoning, or logic, to explain the unknown. In his conclusion, he says that everyone jumping at once in the same place would have "little effect" on the planet. But then some terrible things would happen. When these billions of people tried to go back to their homes, they would run out of food, water, and fuel. They would probably become violent and die "within weeks." Munroe paints an ugly picture, but it's where his reasoning takes him. He ends by stating certainly, "at least now we know."

5   Donna O'Meara could have been hurt as she tried to find answers to her questions about volcanoes, but her wish to learn more and help others kept her pushing forward. Curiosity and intelligence help Roy get through the experience of being bullied. Randall Munroe's logic leads him to conquer feelings of uncertainty about a frightening event. Each person or character is motivated by a desire to know something for certain. Even though none of them is sure what will happen next, they are all motivated into action. As a result, they learn something about themselves and the world.

✏ WRITE

Writers often take notes about their ideas before they sit down to write. Think about what you've learned so far about informative writing to help you begin prewriting.

- Which three individuals from this unit will you focus on in your informative text?

- What steps did they take in order to move forward even when they felt uncertain?

- Were there any cause and effect relationships that set each individual's story in motion?

- How will you compare and contrast each individual's situation?

- Which texts will you use to support your ideas? Will you need to do more research?

Response Instructions

Use the questions in the bulleted list to write a one-paragraph summary. Your summary should describe what your informative essay will be about.

Don't worry about including all of the details now; focus only on the most essential and important elements. You will refer back to this short summary as you continue through the steps of the writing process.

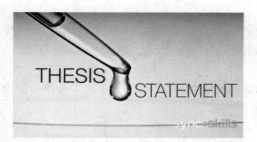

Skill:
Thesis Statement

••• CHECKLIST FOR THESIS STATEMENT

Before you begin writing your thesis statement, ask yourself the following questions:

- What is the prompt asking me to write about?
- What is the topic of my essay?
- What claim do I want to make about the topic of this essay? Is my opinion clear to my reader?
- Does my thesis statement introduce the body of my essay?
- Where should I place my thesis statement?

Here are some methods to introduce and develop your claim and topic:

- think about the topic and central idea of your essay
  - > the central idea of an argument is stated as a claim, or what will be proven or shown to be true
  - > identify as many claims as you intend to prove

- write a clear statement about the central idea or claim. Your thesis statement should:
  - > let the reader anticipate the body of your essay
  - > respond completely to the writing prompt

- consider the best placement for your thesis statement
  - > if your response is short, you may want to get right to the point. Your thesis statement may be presented in the first sentence of the essay.
  - > if your response is longer (as in a formal essay), you can build up your thesis statement. In this case, you can place your thesis statement at the end of your introductory paragraph.

YOUR TURN

Read the excerpts from *Donna O'Meara: Volcano Lady* below. Then, complete the chart by sorting them into those that are thesis statements and those that are not. Write your answer in the second column.

Excerpts	Thesis Statement or Not Thesis Statement?
When Donna went back to school at the age of 32 to study science, her passion for volcanoes began.	
For over 25 years, she has worked with Steve to photograph and study volcanoes all over the world. They hope their documentation will someday be a written and visual record of information that helps scientists to better predict volcanic eruptions.	
Donna says the experience of being stranded on Mt. Stromboli for one freezing night was the scariest experience of her life.	
The following year, she and Steve were married on lava that had oozed from Kilauea on Hawaii and hardened. Lava that hardens creates new landforms, and some volcanoes, such as Surtsey off the coast of Iceland, actually create new islands!	

 WRITE

Use the list and questions from the checklist to write a thesis statement for your essay.

Please note that excerpts and passages in the StudySync® library and this workbook are intended as touchstones to generate interest in an author's work. The excerpts and passages do not substitute for the reading of entire texts, and StudySync® strongly recommends that students seek out and purchase the whole literary or informational work in order to experience it as the author intended. Links to online resellers are available in our digital library. In addition, complete works may be ordered through an authorized reseller by filling out and returning to StudySync® the order form enclosed in this workbook.

Reading & Writing Companion   83

Skill:
Organizing Informative Writing

••• CHECKLIST FOR ORGANIZING INFORMATIVE WRITING

As you consider how to organize your writing for your informative essay, use the following questions as a guide:

- What is my topic? How can I summarize the main idea?

- What is the logical order of my ideas, concepts, and information? Do I see a pattern that is similar to a specific text structure?

- Which organizing structure should I use to present my information?

- How might using graphics, headings, or some form of multimedia help to present my information?

Here are some strategies to help you organize ideas, concepts, and information and aid comprehension:

- definition is useful for:
  - > defining a difficult idea or concept

  - > defining the essential qualities of a subject

  - > teaching readers about a topic or how to do something

  - > providing examples

  - > restating a definition in different ways to help readers understand the subject

- classification is useful for:
  - > dividing larger ideas and concepts into subcategories that are easier to understand

  - > sorting information into subcategories

  - > using subcategories to clarify ideas and provide detailed descriptions

- compare and contrast is useful for:
  - > comparing the similarities and differences between two texts, ideas, or concepts

- cause and effect is useful for:
  - > explaining what and why something happened

  - > understanding how things change over time

 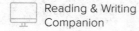

- visual elements

  > use headings to organize your essay into groups of information

  > use graphics, such as charts or tables, to visually represent large amounts of information

  > use multimedia, such as video, sound, and hypertext links, to help readers understand complex ideas and concepts

YOUR TURN

Read the thesis statements and descriptions of each writer's overall purpose for writing below. Then, complete the chart by writing the organizational structure that would best develop the thesis and achieve the writer's overall purpose.

Organizational Structure Options

Cause and Effect   Steps in a Process in Sequential Order   Compare and Contrast   Problem and Solution

Thesis	Purpose	Organizational Structure
The Civil War reshaped American ideas about freedom by resolving the question of slavery.	to show how the Civil War caused Americans to change the way they think about freedom	
Although many people prefer cats, some people find dogs to be the best companions.	to show the differences and similarities between cat ownership and dog ownership	
Bullying is a serious issue for some students, but with support from teachers, parents, and administrators, we can eliminate the problem.	to present a possible solution for the problem of bullying in schools	
The Hudson River is the longest glacial river in America, and the way it was formed is quite fascinating.	to explain how the Hudson River was formed	

 WRITE

Use the steps in the checklist to plan out the organization of your informative essay.

Skill:
Supporting Details

As you look for supporting details to develop your topic, claim, or thesis statement, ask yourself the following questions:

- What is my main idea about this topic?
- What does a reader need to know about the topic in order to understand the main idea?
- What details will support my thesis?
- Is this information necessary to the reader's understanding of the topic?
- Does this information help to develop and refine my key concept or idea?
- Does this information relate closely to my thesis or claim?
- Where can I find better evidence that will provide stronger support for my point?

Here are some suggestions for how you can develop your topic:

- review your thesis or claim
- consider your main idea
- note what the reader will need to know in order to understand the topic
- be sure to consult credible sources
- use different types of supporting details, such as:

  > facts that are specific to your topic and enhance your discussion to establish credibility with your reader and build information

  > definitions to explain difficult concepts, terms, or ideas in your topic, claim, or thesis statement

  > concrete details that will add descriptive and detailed material to your topic

  > quotations to directly connect your thesis statement or claim to the text

  > examples and other information to deepen your claim, topic, or thesis statement

YOUR TURN

Choose the best answer to each question.

1. The following is a section from a previous draft of Colin's essay. Colin would like to add a sentence to support the idea that he has presented in the underlined sentence. Which of these would BEST follow and support the underlined sentence?

> In "Everybody Jump," scientist Randall Munroe is motivated to use logic to answer a difficult question: "What would happen if everyone on earth stood as close to each other as they could and jumped . . . at the same instant?" <u>He knows that this could never really happen, but Munroe takes the question seriously.</u>

- ○ A. He knows that other people are curious about this topic and uncertain about the answer.
- ○ B. It's an interesting scenario, even if it can't happen in real life.
- ○ C. It's a chance for him to impress readers with his ability to use mathematical reasoning to solve real-life problems.
- ○ D. He hopes to advance the science of kinematics.

2. The following is a paragraph from a previous draft of Colin's informative essay. Colin has included an irrelevant sentence in the paragraph. Which sentence should be deleted from this paragraph?

> (1) Roy is motivated by a desire for knowledge. (2) He's also clever at dealing with problems. (3) These qualities help Roy—who's the new kid at school—deal with Dana the bully. (4) Roy's family has recently moved from Montana to Florida. (5) Dana is attacking Roy on the way to school when Roy sees a boy running past the school bus. (6) Even though Dana is hurting him, Roy is curious about the boy: "Who was he? What was he running from?" (7) Roy doesn't care about the pain. (8) He just wants Dana to stop bothering him. (9) When Roy tells Dana "I've had enough," Dana lets him go. (10) Now Roy is free to wonder about the strange boy.

- ○ A. Sentence 2
- ○ B. Sentence 4
- ○ C. Sentence 6
- ○ D. Sentence 9

 WRITE

Use the steps and questions in the checklist to revise the body of your informative essay.

Informative Writing Process: Draft

PLAN	DRAFT	REVISE	EDIT AND PUBLISH

You have already made progress toward writing your informative essay. Now it is time to draft your informative essay.

✏ WRITE

Use your Plan and other responses in your Binder to draft your informative essay. You may also have new ideas as you begin drafting. Feel free to explore those new ideas as they occur to you. You can also ask yourself these questions:

☐ Does my essay fully address the prompt?

☐ Have I included a clear thesis statement or controlling idea?

☐ Does my thesis statement let readers know what to expect in the body of my essay?

☐ Does the organizational text structure support my purpose for writing? Would another text structure be more effective?

Before you submit your draft, read it over carefully. You want to be sure you've responded to all aspects of the prompt.

Please note that excerpts and passages in the StudySync® library and this workbook are intended as touchstones to generate interest in an author's work. The excerpts and passages do not substitute for the reading of entire texts, and StudySync® strongly recommends that students seek out and purchase the whole literary or informational work in order to experience it as the author intended. Links to online resellers are available in our digital library. In addition, complete works may be ordered through an authorized reseller by filling out and returning to StudySync® the order form enclosed in this workbook.

Reading & Writing Companion **89**

Here is Colin's informative essay draft. As you read, identify how effectively he has presented his thesis statement or controlling idea and organized his information.

STUDENT MODEL: FIRST DRAFT

Skill:
Introductions

By adding a "hook" to his introduction, Colin has made his essay more interesting to readers. He has also made his thesis more concise while keeping important details.

Skill:
Precise Language

Colin notices that he's using some inexact words. He replaces the phrase "triumph over" with the more precise word "conquer."

Skill:
Style

In order to make his writing have an academic tone, Colin decides to replace the words "scary job" with more sophisticated vocabulary, such as "the unknown and hazardous world of volcanoes."

~~Scientist Donna O'Meara is motivated by a desire to understand something dangerous. She also wants to help others. The character Roy in Carl Hiaasen's book Hoot is motivated by curiosity. His quick-witted thinking helps him out. Author Randall Munroe is motivated by mathematical reasoning to answer what seems to be an impossible question. Each of these people or characters has a different motivation. Each of them faces different obstacles and problems. But each of them learns something important.~~

Sometimes people are motivated to take action without really knowing why. It could be a feeling, a goal, or a person that encourages them. Scientist Donna O'Meara is motivated by a desire to understand something dangerous. She also wants to help others. The character Roy in Carl Hiaasen's book *Hoot* is motivated by curiosity. His quick-witted thinking helps him out. Author Randall Munroe is motivated by mathematical reasoning. He wants to answer what seems to be an impossible question. Each of these people or characters has a different motivation and faces different obstacles and problems, but they all learn something important.

~~Donna O'Meara's desire to understand how volcanoes work has some-times put her in danger. Most people would probably be afraid to get close to a volcano. There's a lot we don't know about them. But O'meara has risked her life to study them. The desire for knowledge has pushed O'Meara to triumph over her scary job. Now she's an expert on volcanoes and shares her knowledge to help keep others safe. She hopes her work will "help (save the lives) of people who live near" volcanoes.~~

Donna O'Meara's desire to understand how volcanoes work has sometimes put her in danger. Most people would probably be afraid to get close to a volcano. There's a lot we don't know about them. But O'Meara has risked her life to study them. During her first visit to a volcano, she dodged "lava bombs," and hot lava melted her shoes. Another time, she and her husband Steve "were trapped on a ledge in the freezing cold with scalding rocks flying around them." The desire for knowledge has pushed O'Meara to conquer the unknown and hazardous world of volcanoes. Now she's an expert on volcanoes. She shares her knowledge to help keep others safe when volcanoes erupt. She hopes her work will "help save the lives of people who live near" volcanoes.

Skill:
Transitions

~~The character Roy is motivated by a desire for knowledge. He's also clever when it comes to dealing with problems. These qualities help Roy who's the new kid at school deal with Dana the bully. Dana is attacking Roy on his way to school, when Roy sees a boy running past the school bus. Roy is "griped with curiousity" about the boy: "... Who was he? What was he runing from?" Roy doesn't care about the pain. He just wants Dana to stop bothering him, and he is smarter than Dana. He does know that Dana is "a well-known [idiot]." Roy also knows that fighting back would be "a complete waste of (energy)." When Roy tells Dana "I've had enough," Dana lets him go. Now Roy, released from the grip of Dana's hands, are free to wonder about the strange boy. Roy's curiousity and his intelligence help him get out of a bad situation~~

Like Donna O'Meara, the character Roy in *Hoot* is motivated by a desire for knowledge. He's also clever when it comes to dealing with problems. These qualities help Roy, who's the new kid at school, deal with Dana the bully. Dana is attacking Roy on his way to school when Roy sees a boy running past the school bus. Even though Dana is hurting him, Roy is "gripped with curiosity" about the boy: "Who was he? What was he running from?" Roy doesn't care about the pain. He just wants Dana to stop bothering him, and he is smarter than Dana. Although Roy might not know the boy running past the bus, he does know that Dana is "a well-known idiot." Roy also knows that fighting back would be "a complete waste of energy." When Roy tells Dana "I've had enough," Dana lets him go. Now Roy, released from the grip of Dana's hands, is free to wonder about the strange boy. Roy's curiosity and his intelligence help him get out of a bad situation.

In "Everybody Jump," scientist Randall Munroe is motivated to use mathematical reasoning to answer a difficult question: "What would happen if everyone on earth stood as close to each other as they

Colin continues to add transitions to his draft in order to clarify ideas between paragraphs and make apparent his organizational structure. He realizes that there is no connection between the paragraph about Donna O'Meara and the one about Roy from Hoot. Therefore, he adds the transitional phrase "Like Donna O'Meara" before introducing the character Roy. Colin also adds cohesion and clarity to the ideas within this paragraph by adding other transitions, such as "Even though Dana is hurting him" and "Although Roy might not know the boy running past the bus."

NOTES

could and jumpped . . . at the same instant?" This could never sucsede in real life since it would totally be unpossible to get everyone in the same place at the same time, but Munroe takes the question seriously. He knows that "many others" are curious about this topic and discertain about the answer. Munroe uses mathematical reasoning, or logic, to explain the inknown. In his conclusion, he says that everyone jumping at once in the same place. Would have "little effect" on the planet. But then some terrible things would happen. When these billions of people tried to go back to their homes, they would be come violent and die "within weeks." Munroe paints an ugly picture, but it's where his reasoning takes him. He ends by stating certainly, "at least now we know."

Donna O'Meara could have been hurt as she tried to find answers to her questions about volcanoes, but her wish to learn more and help others kept her pushing forward. Curiosity and intelligence help Roy get through the experience of being bullied. Randall Munroe's logic leads him to conquer feelings of uncertainty about a frightening event. Each person or character is motivated by a desire to know something for certain. Even though none of them is sure what will happen next, they are all motivated into action. As a result, they learn something about themselves and the world.

Skill:
Conclusions

Colin decides that his conclusion does a good job of wrapping up his main points about each person. However, he realizes that he has not rephrased his main idea, or thesis. Thus, he adds several sentences that show his depth of knowledge about his main idea.

Skill:
Introductions

Before you write your introduction, ask yourself the following questions:

- What is my claim? How can I introduce my claim(s) so it is clear to my reader?

- What is the best way to organize my ideas, concepts, reasons, and evidence in a clear and logical order?

- How will you "hook" your reader's interest? You might:

  > start with an attention-grabbing statement

  > begin with an intriguing question

  > use descriptive words to set a scene

Below are two strategies to help you introduce your topic and claim, and organize reasons and evidence clearly in an introduction:

- Peer Discussion

  > talk about your topic with a partner, explaining what you already know and your ideas about your topic

  > write notes about the ideas you have discussed and any new questions you may have

  > review your notes and think about what will be your claim or controlling idea

  > briefly state your claim or thesis

  > organize your reasons and evidence in an order that is clear to readers, presenting your reasons first, followed by evidence

  > write a possible "hook"

- Freewriting

  > freewrite for 10 minutes about your topic. Don't worry about grammar, punctuation, or having fully formed ideas. The point of freewriting is to discover ideas.

  > review your notes and think about what will be your claim or controlling idea

> briefly state your claim or thesis

> organize your reasons and evidence in an order that is clear to readers, presenting your reasons first, followed by evidence

> write a possible "hook"

YOUR TURN

Choose the best answer to each question.

1. Below is the introduction from a previous draft of Colin's essay. The first sentence is a weak "hook." How could Colin rewrite the sentence to better grab the reader's attention?

> <u>Lots of things motivate people.</u> Scientist Donna O'Meara is motivated to understand volcanoes, even if it means putting herself in danger. Roy in Carl Hiaasen's novel *Hoot* is motivated by curiosity. Author Randall Munroe is motivated by the challenge of using mathematical reasoning to answer a seemingly impossible question.

- ○ A. People are motivated by different things.
- ○ B. A quest for understanding, a keen sense of curiosity, a sharp mind—many different things motivate people to act.
- ○ C. Motivation comes from surprising places.
- ○ D. Motivation—the reason or reasons that drive people to take action—comes from many sources.

2. Colin wants to improve the introduction in an earlier draft of his informative essay. Which of these revisions to the following three sentences makes a more concise thesis?

> Each of these people or characters has a different motivation. Each of them faces different obstacles and problems. But each of them learns something important.

- ○ A. Each person learns something important through a different motivation.
- ○ B. In each case, they all learn something different.
- ○ C. Despite unique motivations and different obstacles, each of them learns something important.
- ○ D. In each case, they face different problems and overcome uncertainty.

 WRITE

Use the questions in the checklist to revise the introduction of your informative essay.

Skill:
Transitions

Before you revise your current draft to include transitions, think about:

- the key ideas you discuss in your body paragraphs

- the organizational structure of your essay

- the relationships among ideas and concepts

Next, reread your current draft and note areas in your essay where:

- the organizational structure is not yet apparent

  > For example, if you are comparing and contrasting two texts, your explanations about how two texts are similar and different should be clearly stated.

- the relationship between ideas from one paragraph to the next is unclear

  > For example, an essay that describes a process in sequential order should make clear the order of steps using transitional words like *first, then, next,* and *finally.*

- the relationship between ideas within a paragraph is unclear

  > For example, when providing evidence to support an idea in a topic sentence, you should introduce the evidence with a transition such as *for example* or *to illustrate.*

Revise your draft to use appropriate transitions to clarify the relationships among ideas and concepts, using the following questions as a guide:

- What kind of transitions should I use to make the organizational structure clear to readers?

- Which transition best connects the ideas within a paragraph?

- Which transition best connects ideas across paragraphs?

YOUR TURN

Choose the best answer to the question.

1. Below is a section from Colin's essay. Which transition would make the most sense to add to the beginning of sentence 3?

> 1. Munroe uses mathematical reasoning, or logic, to explain the unknown. 2. In his conclusion, he says that everyone jumping at once in the same place would have "little effect" on the planet. 3. Some terrible things would happen.

○ A. However,
○ B. To illustrate,
○ C. In addition,
○ D. Finally,

 YOUR TURN

Complete the chart by adding the following transitions to sentences of your informative essay.

Transition	Rewritten Sentence
However	
To illustrate	
In addition	
For example	

Please note that excerpts and passages in the StudySync® library and this workbook are intended as touchstones to generate interest in an author's work. The excerpts and passages do not substitute for the reading of entire texts, and StudySync® strongly recommends that students seek out and purchase the whole literary or informational work in order to experience it as the author intended. Links to online resellers are available in our digital library. In addition, complete works may be ordered through an authorized reseller by filling out and returning to StudySync® the order form enclosed in this workbook.

Reading & Writing Companion   **97**

Skill:
Precise Language

As you consider precise language and domain-specific vocabulary related to a subject or topic, use the following questions as a guide:

- What information am I trying to convey or explain to my audience?

- Are there any key concepts that need to be explained or understood?

- What domain-specific vocabulary is relevant to my topic and explanation?

- Where can I use more precise vocabulary in my explanation?

Here are some suggestions that will help guide you in using precise language and domain-specific vocabulary to inform about or explain a topic:

- determine the topic or area of study you will be writing about

- identify key concepts that need explanation in order to inform readers

- research any domain-specific vocabulary that you may need to define

- substitute vague, general, or overused words and phrases for more precise, descriptive, and domain-specific language

- reread your writing to refine and revise if needed

YOUR TURN

Choose the best answer to the question.

1. Below is a section from a previous draft of Colin's essay. How could Colin change sentence 2 to add more precise language?

> 1. In "Everybody Jump," scientist Randall Munroe is motivated to use mathematical reasoning to answer a difficult question: "What would happen if everyone on earth stood as close to each other as they could and jumped . . . at the same instant?" 2. This could never happen in real life, but Munroe takes the question seriously.

- ○ A. This could never happen in fantasy, but Munroe takes the question seriously.
- ○ B. This could never happen in reality, but Munroe considers the query seriously.
- ○ C. This could never happen in real life, but Munroe takes the debate seriously.
- ○ D. This could never happen in real life, but Munroe takes the question totally seriously.

 YOUR TURN

Complete the chart by adding an example of precise language and domain-specific language to your essay.

Type of Language	Rewritten Sentence
precise language	
domain-specific vocabulary	

Please note that excerpts and passages in the StudySync® library and this workbook are intended as touchstones to generate interest in an author's work. The excerpts and passages do not substitute for the reading of entire texts, and StudySync® strongly recommends that students seek out and purchase the whole literary or informational work in order to experience it as the author intended. Links to online resellers are available in our digital library. In addition, complete works may be ordered through an authorized reseller by filling out and returning to StudySync® the order form enclosed in this workbook.

Reading & Writing Companion 99

Skill:
Style

••• CHECKLIST FOR STYLE

First, reread the draft of your informative essay and identify the following:

- places where you use slang, contractions, abbreviations, and a conversational tone

- areas where you could use subject-specific or academic language in order to help persuade or inform your readers

- moments where you use first-person (*I*) or second person (*you*)

- areas where sentence structure lacks variety

- incorrect uses of the conventions of standard English for grammar, spelling, capitalization, and punctuation

Establish and maintain a formal style in your essay, using the following questions as a guide:

- Have I avoided slang in favor of academic language?

- Did I consistently use a third-person point of view, using third-person pronouns (*he, she, they*)?

- Have I varied my sentence structure and the length of my sentences? Apply these specific questions where appropriate:

  > Where should I make some sentences longer by using conjunctions to connect independent clauses, dependent clauses, and phrases?

  > Where should I make some sentences shorter by separating any independent clauses?

- Did I follow the conventions of standard English, including:

  > grammar?

  > spelling?

  > capitalization?

  > punctuation?

YOUR TURN

Choose the best answer to the question.

1. Below is a section from a previous draft of Colin's essay. Which of the following revisions shows correct conventions of English?

> Now Roy, released from the grip of Dana's hands, are free to wonder about the strange boy. Roy's curiousity and his intelligence help him get out of a bad situation.

○ A. Now Roy released from the grip of Dana's hands is free to wonder about the strange boy. Roy's curiosity and his intelligence help him get out of a bad situation.

○ B. Now Roy, released from the grip of Dana's hands, is free to wonder about the strange boy. Roy's curiosity and him intelligence help he get out of a bad situation.

○ C. Now Roy, released from the grip of Dana's hands, is free to wonder about the strange boy and Roy's curiosity and his intelligence help him get out of a bad situation.

○ D. Now Roy, released from the grip of Dana's hands, is free to wonder about the strange boy. Roy's curiosity and his intelligence help him get out of a bad situation.

YOUR TURN

Complete the chart by making style changes within your informative essay.

Style Change	Rewritten Sentence
Eliminate slang, contractions, abbreviations, or a conversational tone.	
Use domain-specific or academic language.	
Vary sentence structure and the length of sentences.	

Skill:
Conclusions

••• CHECKLIST FOR CONCLUSIONS

Before you write your conclusion, ask yourself the following questions:

- How can I restate the thesis or main idea in my concluding section or statement? What impression can I make on my reader?

- How can I write my conclusion so that it follows logically from the information I presented?

- Have I left out any important information in my concluding statement that I have presented in my essay?

Below are two strategies to help you provide a concluding statement or section that follows from the information or explanation presented:

- Peer Discussion

  > after you have written your introduction and body paragraphs, talk with a partner and tell them what you want readers to remember, writing notes about your discussion

  > review your notes and think about what you wish to express in your conclusion

  > do not simply restate your claim or thesis statement. Rephrase your main idea to show the depth of your knowledge.

  > write your conclusion

- Freewriting

  > freewrite for 10 minutes about what you might include in your conclusion. Don't worry about grammar, punctuation, or having fully formed ideas. The point of freewriting is to discover ideas.

  > review your notes and think about what you wish to express in your conclusion

  > do not simply restate your claim or thesis statement. Rephrase your main idea to show the depth of your knowledge.

  > write your conclusion

YOUR TURN

Choose the best answer to each question.

1. Below is the conclusion from a previous draft of Colin's essay. What key component is Colin missing from his conclusion?

> Donna O'Meara could have been hurt as she tried to find answers to her questions about volcanoes, but her wish to learn more and help others kept her pushing forward. Curiosity and intelligence help Roy get through the experience of being bullied. Randall Munroe's logic leads him to conquer feelings of uncertainty about a frightening event.

- ○ A. restating all three people or characters
- ○ B. restating the essay's thesis
- ○ C. a "hook"
- ○ D. descriptions of the motivation of each person or character

2. Colin wants to improve the conclusion to an earlier draft of his informative essay. What is the most effective revision to make to the underlined sentence in order to end with a memorable comment that expresses the essay's thesis?

> Donna O'Meara could be hurt trying to understand volcanoes, but her wish to learn more spurs her on. Curiosity helps Roy cope with being bullied. Randall Munroe's logic leads him to overcome uncertainty about a frightening event. <u>In each case, the person or character learns something.</u>

- ○ A. In each case, the person learns something important through motivation.
- ○ B. In each case, the desire to push past uncertainty leads to knowledge about themselves and the world.
- ○ C. In each case, the desire to know something pushes the person or character past uncertainty to learn something about themselves and the world.
- ○ D. In each case, knowledge of the world helps them overcome uncertainty.

 WRITE

Use the questions in the checklist to revise the conclusion of your informative essay.

Informative Writing Process: Revise

PLAN	DRAFT	REVISE	EDIT AND PUBLISH

You have written a draft of your informative essay. You have also received input from your peers about how to improve it. Now you are going to revise your draft.

◀◀ REVISION GUIDE

Examine your draft to find areas for revision. Keep in mind your purpose and audience as you revise for clarity, development, organization, and style. Use the guide below to help you review:

Review	Revise	Example
Clarity		
Highlight any place in your essay where there are unnecessary details that lack a formal style and hinder clarity.	Remove irrelevant information and informal language from sentences.	This could never happen in real life ~~since it would totally be impossible to get everyone in the same place at the same time~~, but Munroe takes the question seriously.
Development		
Identify places where you give details in support of your thesis. Note reasons, descriptions, and examples you could incorporate to add support.	Focus on a single idea and add reasons, descriptions, or examples to support your idea.	In his conclusion, he says that everyone jumping at once in the same place would have "little effect" on the planet. But then some terrible things would happen. When these billions of people tried to go back to their homes, they would run out of food, water, and fuel. They ~~they~~ would become violent and die "within weeks."

Review	Revise	Example
Organization		
Review whether your text structure supports your purpose. Annotate places where the organization can be improved.	Rewrite the transition between paragraphs to make the text structure clear to readers.	She shares her knowledge to help keep others safe when volcanoes erupt. She hopes her work will "help save the lives of people who live near" volcanoes. Like Donna O'Meara, the ~~The~~ character Roy is motivated by a desire for knowledge. He's also clever when it comes to dealing with problems.
Style: Word Choice		
Identify prefixes in your writing (such as *in-* and *un-*).	Select sentences to rewrite using correct prefixes.	Munroe uses mathematical reasoning, or logic, to explain the ~~inknown~~ unknown.
Style: Sentence Variety		
Review your essay for precise language. Create comprehensible sentences by using language that is specific to the text.	Rewrite sentences to include domain-specific vocabulary.	The desire for knowledge has pushed O'Meara to conquer ~~her scary job~~ the unknown and hazardous world of volcanoes.

✏ WRITE

Use the guide above, as well as your peer reviews, to help you evaluate your informative essay to determine areas that should be revised.

Please note that excerpts and passages in the StudySync® library and this workbook are intended as touchstones to generate interest in an author's work. The excerpts and passages do not substitute for the reading of entire texts, and StudySync® strongly recommends that students seek out and purchase the whole literary or informational work in order to experience it as the author intended. Links to online resellers are available in our digital library. In addition, complete works may be ordered through an authorized reseller by filling out and returning to StudySync® the order form enclosed in this workbook.

Reading & Writing Companion 105

Informative Writing Process: Edit And Publish

| PLAN | DRAFT | REVISE | EDIT AND PUBLISH |

You have revised your informative essay based on your peer feedback and your own examination.

Now, it is time to edit your informative essay. When you revised, you focused on the content of your essay. You probably looked at your essay's thesis statement, introduction, organizational text structure, supporting details, transitions, precise language, style, and conclusion. When you edit, you focus on the mechanics of your essay, and pay close attention to things like grammar and punctuation.

Use the checklist below to guide you as you edit:

☐ Have I correctly used parentheses, brackets, and ellipses?

☐ Have I correctly used prefixes?

☐ Did I follow spelling rules, especially regarding doubled consonants, compound words, and words ending with the "seed" sound?

☐ Do I have any sentence fragments or run-on sentences?

☐ Have I spelled everything correctly?

Notice some edits Colin has made:

- Corrected the incorrect use of parentheses.

- Corrected incorrect prefixes.

- Used basic spelling rules to correct spelling errors, especially in words with doubled consonants and compound words.

- Changed a verb so that it matches the subject.

- Corrected a sentence fragment.

Roy also knows that fighting back would be "a complete waste of ~~(energy)~~ energy." When Roy tells Dana "I've had enough," Dana lets him go. Now Roy, released from the grip of Dana's hands, ~~are~~ is free to wonder about the strange boy. Roy's ~~curiousity~~ curiosity and his intelligence help him get out of a bad situation.

In "Everybody Jump," scientist Randall Munroe is motivated to use mathematical reasoning to answer a difficult question: "What would happen if everyone on earth stood as close to each other as they could and ~~jumpped~~ jumped . . . at the same instant?" This could never happen in real life, but Munroe takes the question seriously. He knows that "many others" are curious about this topic and ~~discertain~~ uncertain about the answer. Munroe uses mathematical reasoning, or logic, to explain the ~~inknown~~ unknown. In his conclusion, he says that everyone jumping at once in the same place. ~~W~~ would have "little effect" on the planet. But then some terrible things would happen. When these billions of people tried to go back to their homes, they would run out of food, water, and fuel. They would probably ~~be come~~ become violent and die "within weeks."

✏ WRITE

Use the questions on the previous page, as well as your peer reviews, to help you evaluate your informative essay to determine areas that need editing. Then edit your essay to correct those errors.

Once you have made all your corrections, you are ready to publish your work. You can distribute your writing to family and friends, hang it on a bulletin board, or post it on your blog. If you publish online, share the link with your family, friends, and classmates.

Please note that excerpts and passages in the StudySync® library and this workbook are intended as touchstones to generate interest in an author's work. The excerpts and passages do not substitute for the reading of entire texts, and StudySync® strongly recommends that students seek out and purchase the whole literary or informational work in order to experience it as the author intended. Links to online resellers are available in our digital library. In addition, complete works may be ordered through an authorized reseller by filling out and returning to StudySync® the order form enclosed in this workbook.

Reading & Writing Companion   **107**

Tracking Down Typhoid Mary

INFORMATIONAL TEXT

Introduction

This true-life mystery tells about a serious illness and the man who tracked down its source. The story is set in the early 1900s, when people were just

V VOCABULARY

mansion

a large and impressive house

thoroughly

completely; in a detailed way

carrier

a person or animal that transmits a disease without suffering from or showing signs of the disease

isolation

the condition of being alone

inspector

someone whose job is to examine something closely

☰ READ

NOTES

1   It was a lovely day in Oyster Bay. The sun was shining. The sky was blue. At Charles Warren's **mansion** on the shore, though, all was not well. Six people in the house were fighting for their lives. All were very ill with symptoms that included a very high fever. One of them was Charles's little daughter.

2   As it turned out, the six people had typhoid fever. In 1906 it was a common illness, found in crowded parts of the city. However, no one had ever seen it in rich Oyster Bay homes. How did it get there? Where had it come from? Charles wanted to know.

3   Charles hired a man named George Soper. George had an unusual job. He was a sanitation engineer. He worked to make buildings cleaner because making them cleaner kept sickness from spreading. Dirty water and dirty hands made germs spread. One of those germs caused typhoid fever. George set to work in the Warrens' house, looking for the cause of disease.

4   George found nothing wrong with the water pipes. Nothing was wrong with the drains. Could bad seafood be making people sick? George checked the kitchen. Everything seemed fresh and clean. He talked to everyone in the household. By spring, he had the answer. He tracked the fever to one woman. She had worked in the house as a cook. She had worked in other homes before that, and people at those homes had become sick. The woman's name was Mary Mallon.

5   Mary had never been sick herself. Others became sick, but she did not. She was a **carrier** of the disease. She did not believe that she had made anyone sick. She was angry. In fact, she chased George away with a fork!

6   Mary was still a cook. Now she worked for a different family. George was worried. Would she make them sick, too? He called the Health Department. An **inspector** came to talk to Mary, but she ran away. Finally, the police picked her up. They took her to a hospital. There, doctors tested her blood. She was loaded with the germ that caused typhoid fever.

7   How did Mary make people sick? The doctors figured it out. Mary made great peach ice cream. She did not wash her hands **thoroughly**, so germs could spread. The peaches were raw, so cooking did not kill the germs.

8   The Health Department locked Mary away in **isolation**. She lived alone on an island for three years. She went to court. The judge agreed that she was dangerous. Finally, in 1910, she was freed.

9   Mary continued to work as a cook. Everywhere she worked, people got sick. Many people got typhoid fever from Mary Mallon. At least three people died from her cooking.

10 In 1915, the courts locked Mary up again. She died on the island 23 years later. She had never once had typhoid fever. Even so, people everywhere called her "Typhoid Mary."

First Read

Read the text. After you read, answer the Think Questions below.

☁ THINK QUESTIONS

1. Whom did Charles Warren hire? Why did he hire that person?

    Charles Warren hired _____.

    He hired him _____.

2. How did Mary get people sick?

    Mary got people sick because _____.

3. What happened to Mary after she was freed in 1910?

    After Mary was freed she _____.

4. Use context to confirm the meaning of the word *isolation* as it is used in "Tracking Down Typhoid Mary." Write your definition of *isolation* here.

    Isolation means _____.

    A context clue is _____.

5. What is another way to say that you cleaned your room *thoroughly*?

    I cleaned my room _____.

Please note that excerpts and passages in the StudySync® library and this workbook are intended as touchstones to generate interest in an author's work. The excerpts and passages do not substitute for the reading of entire texts, and StudySync® strongly recommends that students seek out and purchase the whole literary or informational work in order to experience it as the author intended. Links to online resellers are available in our digital library. In addition, complete works may be ordered through an authorized reseller by filling out and returning to StudySync® the order form enclosed in this workbook.

Reading & Writing Companion   **111**

Skill:
Language Structures

★ DEFINE

In every language, there are rules that tell how to **structure** sentences. These rules define the correct order of words. In the English language, for example, a **basic** structure for sentences is subject, verb, and object. Some sentences have more **complicated** structures.

You will encounter both basic and complicated **language structures** in the classroom materials you read. Being familiar with language structures will help you better understand the text.

••• CHECKLIST FOR LANGUAGE STRUCTURES

To improve your comprehension of language structures, do the following:

✓ Monitor your understanding.

- Ask yourself: Why do I not understand this sentence? Is it because I do not understand some of the words? Or is it because I do not understand the way the words are ordered in the sentence?

✓ Pay attention to verbs followed by prepositions.

- A **verb** names an action.

  > Example: I **sit** on my chair.

  > This tells the reader what the subject of the sentence is doing (sitting).

- A **preposition** defines the relationship between two or more nouns or verbs in a sentence.

  > Example: I sit **on** my chair.

  > This tells the reader where the subject is doing the action (on a chair).

- Sometimes the preposition comes directly after the verb, but it can also be separated by another word.

    Example: I **took** it **to** school with me.

- Sometimes the preposition changes the meaning of the verb. This is called a **phrasal verb**.

    > Example: The teacher liked to **call on** the students in the front of the class.

    > The phrasal verb *call on* means "to select someone to share information."

✓ Break down the sentence into its parts.

- Ask yourself: What words make up the verbs in this sentence? Is the verb followed by a preposition? How does this affect the meaning of the sentence?

✓ Confirm your understanding with a peer or teacher.

Please note that excerpts and passages in the StudySync® library and this workbook are intended as touchstones to generate interest in an author's work. The excerpts and passages do not substitute for the reading of entire texts, and StudySync® strongly recommends that students seek out and purchase the whole literary or informational work in order to experience it as the author intended. Links to online resellers are available in our digital library. In addition, complete works may be ordered through an authorized reseller by filling out and returning to StudySync® the order form enclosed in this workbook.

Reading & Writing
Companion

113

⟳ YOUR TURN

Read each sentence from the text. Find the verb and preposition that goes along with it. Then, write the verb in the center column and the preposition in the last column. Remember, the preposition may not always directly follow the verb.

Sentences	Verbs	Prepositions
At least three people died from her cooking.		
He tracked the fever to one woman.		
She lived alone on an island for three years.		
She went to court.		

Skill:
Main Ideas and Details

★ DEFINE

The **main ideas** are the most important ideas of a paragraph, a section, or an entire text. The **supporting details** are details that describe or explain the main ideas.

To **distinguish** between the main ideas and the supporting details, you will need to decide what information is the most important and supports or explains the main ideas.

••• CHECKLIST FOR MAIN IDEAS AND DETAILS

In order to distinguish between main ideas and supporting details, do the following:

✓ Preview the text. Look at headings, topic sentences, and boldface vocabulary.

• Ask yourself: What seems to be the main idea in this text?

✓ Read the text.

• Ask yourself: What are the most important ideas? What details support or explain the most important ideas?

✓ Take notes or use a graphic organizer to distinguish between main ideas and supporting details.

YOUR TURN

Read the following excerpt from the text. Then, complete the multiple-choice questions below.

---

from **"Tracking Down Typhoid Mary"**

How did Mary make people sick? The doctors figured it out. Mary made great peach ice cream. She did not wash her hands thoroughly, so germs could spread. The peaches were raw, so cooking did not kill the germs.

---

1. What is the main idea of the paragraph?

   ○ A. Mary never learned to clean her tools.
   ○ B. Mary wanted to make people sick.
   ○ C. Mary's peach ice cream made people sick.
   ○ D. Mary's ice cream needed further cooking.

2. Which detail supports the main idea?

   ○ A. Mary made great ice cream.
   ○ B. Cooking did not kill the germs.
   ○ C. Peaches may be used in ice cream.
   ○ D. Germs spread when Mary washed up.

3. Which other detail supports the main idea of the paragraph?

   ○ A. Mary did not wash her hands properly.
   ○ B. Peaches are often loaded with germs.
   ○ C. Mary forgot to cook the peaches.
   ○ D. Ice cream can cause stomach pains.

TRACKING
DOWN
TYPHOID
MARY

Close Read

 WRITE

PERSONAL RESPONSE: Imagine that you were Mary Mallon in this story. How would you feel about George? How would you react to being told you were spreading disease, and why? Write about your experience as Mary. Recount details from the original story in your response. Pay attention to spelling patterns and rules as you write.

Use the checklist below to guide you as you write.

☐ How do you think Mary Mallon feels?

☐ Why does George look for Mary?

☐ What information from the text supports your ideas?

Use the sentence frames to organize and write your personal response.

Mary is not sure why George _____.

I would feel _____ if _____.

I think I would _____.

Spreading germs is bad because _____.

I practice healthy habits to _____.

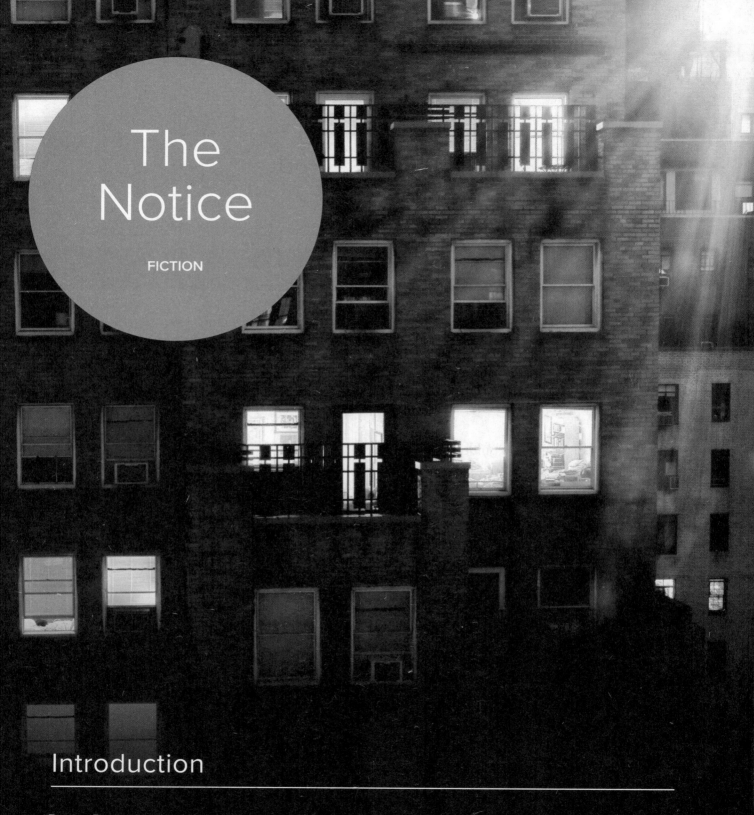

The Notice

FICTION

Introduction

New York City in the 1930s was home to immigrant families who traveled there from every corner of the world in search of a happy life. At times, they faced a less-than-warm welcome. In the story "The Notice," two Czech families experience a dilemma: can they keep their livelihood when their landlord prefers not to rent to immigrants?

V VOCABULARY

impatient

unwilling to wait for someone or something

property

a piece of land or a building that is owned by a person or business

counter

a flat surface over which goods are bought or food is served.

admit

to tell the truth, but in an unwilling way

glassware

objects made of glass

☰ READ

NOTES

1   The last customer put on her coat and left. It was a cold January night. My táta locked the door and looked out. He stood there for a while. I began to grow **impatient**. I wanted to see his warm smile. I saw that smile every day, after he closed our shop for the day.

2   He turned at last, but he didn't look happy. He placed his hand on my shoulder and walked past me.

3   My *máma* and I watched him stand behind the **counter**. He took out a folded piece of paper from a small wooden box. He spread the paper out before him. Delicate glass vases, bowls, and plates sparkled in the display case below. Our family and the Vaceks made them in the back of the shop. We used to make the same **glassware** in Prague. The Vaceks were watching my táta too.

4   "What can we do, Dominik?" Josefa asked. Her husband, Miroslav, winced slightly.

5   Eventually my *táta* looked up. Josefa's question brought him back from some faraway place.

6   "Mr. Davis hasn't given us much of a choice." There was anger in his voice. "He has already made his choice. He will give our shop to anyone who didn't pass through Ellis Island. Or, he will *allow* us to pay extra for letting us work on his **property**."

7   *Máma* knew what my *táta* said was true.

8   *Táta* gripped the edges of the display case. Like the glassware the case contained, his expression was easy for everyone to see.

9   Mr. Vacek read the notice again. Mr. Davis left it on our shop door this morning. He didn't even hand it to my *táta* or Mr. Vacek.

10   I glanced at it. Mr. Davis blamed the doubling of our rent on hard times. It was difficult to imagine that he knew about hard times.

11   Mr. Vacek cleared his throat and said, "Josefa and I, we need this place." He didn't want to **admit** it, but it was true.

12   My *táta* looked at Mr. Vacek and nodded. They had known each other since they were children. My *táta* didn't want to hear his friend say that. But I knew my *táta* wasn't going to abandon him now.

13   "Whatever we decide, we will decide it together," my táta said.

First Read

Read the text. After you read, answer the Think Questions below.

☁ THINK QUESTIONS

1. Who are the main characters in the story? What is their relationship?

   The main characters are _____.

   They are _____.

2. Write two or three sentences describing the setting of the story.

   The setting _____.

   _____.

3. At the end of the story, why does the narrator still have hope?

   The narrator still has hope because _____.

4. Use context to confirm the meaning of the word *admit* as it is used in "The Notice." Write your definition of *admit* here.

   Admit means _____.

   A context clue is _____.

5. What is another way to say the word *abandon*?

   Another way to say *abandon* is _____.

Skill:
Analyzing Expressions

★ DEFINE

When you read, you may find English expressions that you do not know. An **expression** is a group of words that communicates an idea. Three types of expressions are idioms, sayings, and figurative language. They can be difficult to understand because the meanings of the words are different from their **literal**, or usual, meanings.

An **idiom** is an expression that is commonly known among a group of people. For example: "It's raining cats and dogs" means it is raining heavily. **Sayings** are short expressions that contain advice or wisdom. For instance: "Don't count your chickens before they hatch" means do not plan on something good happening before it happens. **Figurative** language is when you describe something by comparing it with something else, either directly (using the words *like* or *as*) or indirectly. For example, "I'm as hungry as a horse" means I'm very hungry. None of these expressions are actual animals.

••• CHECKLIST FOR ANALYZING EXPRESSIONS

To determine the meaning of an expression, remember the following:

✓ If you find a confusing group of words, it may be an expression. The meaning of words in expressions may not be their literal meaning.

  • Ask yourself: Is this confusing because the words are new? Or because the words do not make sense together?

✓ Determining the overall meaning may require that you use one or more of the following:

  • context clues

  • a dictionary or other resource

  • teacher or peer support

✓ Highlight important information before and after the expression to look for clues.

YOUR TURN

Read paragraphs 5–6 and 10–11 from the text. Then complete the multiple-choice questions below.

---

from **"The Notice"**

Eventually my *táta* looked up. Josefa's question brought him back from some faraway place.

"Mr. Davis hasn't given us much of a choice." There was anger in his voice. "He has already made his choice. He will give our shop to anyone who didn't pass through Ellis Island. Or, he will allow us to pay extra for letting us work on his property."

. . .

I glanced at it. Mr. Davis blamed the doubling of our rent on hard times. It was difficult to imagine that he knew about hard times.

Mr. Vacek cleared his throat and said, "Josefa and I, we need this place." He didn't want to admit it, but it was true.

---

1. What does the narrator mean by "brought him back from a faraway place" in paragraph 5?

    ○ A. He came back from a distant country.
    ○ B. Josefa brought *táta* from a distant place.
    ○ C. Josefa's question rescued *táta*.
    ○ D. The question brought *táta's* attention back.

2. Which context clue helped you determine the meaning of the expression?

    ○ A. "Mr. Davis hasn't given us much of a choice."
    ○ B. "He has already made his choice."
    ○ C. "There was anger in his voice."
    ○ D. "...Eventually my *táta* looked up..."

Please note that excerpts and passages in the StudySync® library and this workbook are intended as touchstones to generate interest in an author's work. The excerpts and passages do not substitute for the reading of entire texts, and StudySync® strongly recommends that students seek out and purchase the whole literary or informational work in order to experience it as the author intended. Links to online resellers are available in our digital library. In addition, complete works may be ordered through an authorized reseller by filling out and returning to StudySync® the order form enclosed in this workbook.

Reading & Writing Companion   **123**

3. What does the narrator mean when she says "hard times" in paragraph 10?

    ○ A. a time where people need money
    ○ B. a strong, solid period of time
    ○ C. events that happened long ago
    ○ D. the due date for paying your bills

4. Which context clue helped you determine the meaning of the expression?

    ○ A. "Josefa and I, we need this place"
    ○ B. "I glanced at it."
    ○ C. "He has already made his choice."
    ○ D. "Mr. Davis blamed the doubling of our rent …"

Skill:
Comparing and Contrasting

★ DEFINE

To **compare** is to show how two or more pieces of information or literary elements in a text are similar. To **contrast** is to show how two or more pieces of information or literary elements in a text are different. By comparing and contrasting, you can better understand the **meaning** and the **purpose** of the text you are reading.

••• CHECKLIST FOR COMPARING AND CONTRASTING

In order to compare and contrast, do the following:

✓ Look for information or elements that you can compare and contrast.

- Ask yourself: How are these two things similar? How are they different?

✓ Look for signal words that indicate a compare-and-contrast relationship.

- Ask yourself: Are there any words that indicate the writer is trying to compare and contrast two or more things?

✓ Use a graphic organizer, such as a Venn diagram or chart, to compare and contrast information.

Please note that excerpts and passages in the StudySync® library and this workbook are intended as touchstones to generate interest in an author's work. The excerpts and passages do not substitute for the reading of entire texts, and StudySync® strongly recommends that students seek out and purchase the whole literary or informational work in order to experience it as the author intended. Links to online resellers are available in our digital library. In addition, complete works may be ordered through an authorized reseller by filling out and returning to StudySync® the order form enclosed in this workbook.

Reading & Writing Companion   **125**

⟳ YOUR TURN

Read the following excerpt from the text. Then complete the Compare-and-Contrast chart by writing the letter of the correct example in chart below.

---

from **"The Notice"**

Mr. Vacek read the notice again. Mr. Davis left it on our shop door this morning. He didn't even hand it to my *táta* or Mr. Vacek.

I glanced at it. Mr. Davis blamed the doubling of our rent on hard times. It was difficult to imagine that he knew about hard times.

Mr. Vacek cleared his throat and said, "Josefa and I, we need this place." He didn't want to admit it, but it was true.

My *táta* looked at Mr. Vacek and nodded. They had known each other since they were children. My *táta* didn't want to hear his friend say that. But I knew my *táta* wasn't going to abandon him now.

Examples	
A	know Mr. Vacek
B	would never abandon his friend
C	left a notice without talking in person

Mr. Davis	Both	Táta

Close Read

✏️ **WRITE**

PERSONAL RESPONSE: Beginning a new life in a new country can be difficult. Imagine that like the families in "The Notice," you are starting over in a new country and trying to find a job. However, even though you are qualified, no one wants to hire you because you weren't born in their country. Think about the types of information you would need to provide in order to prove that you are able to do the work. Explain why that information is important. Pay attention to verb tenses as you write.

Use the checklist below to guide you as you write.

☐ What is a time when you were treated unfairly?

☐ How did you feel?

☐ What did you do?

☐ How does your experience compare to the families in "The Notice"?

☐ How does your experience contrast to the families in "The Notice"?

Use the sentence frames to organize and write your personal response.

I was once treated unfairly when _____.

It made me feel _____ because _____.

My experience is like the story "The Notice" because _____.

Unlike in the story, I _____.

Please note that excerpts and passages in the StudySync® library and this workbook are intended as touchstones to generate interest in an author's work. The excerpts and passages do not substitute for the reading of entire texts, and StudySync® strongly recommends that students seek out and purchase the whole literary or informational work in order to experience it as the author intended. Links to online resellers are available in our digital library. In addition, complete works may be ordered through an authorized reseller by filling out and returning to StudySync® the order form enclosed in this workbook.

Reading & Writing Companion   **127**

studysync®

Text Fulfillment Through StudySync

If you are interested in specific titles, please fill out the form below and we will check availability through our partners.

ORDER DETAILS

Date:

TITLE	AUTHOR	Paperback/ Hardcover	Specific Edition *If Applicable*	Quantity

SHIPPING INFORMATION

Contact:

Title:

School/District:

Address Line 1:

Address Line 2:

Zip or Postal Code:

Phone:

Mobile:

Email:

BILLING INFORMATION   ☐ *SAME AS SHIPPING*

Contact:

Title:

School/District:

Address Line 1:

Address Line 2:

Zip or Postal Code:

Phone:

Mobile:

Email:

PAYMENT INFORMATION

☐ CREDIT CARD

Name on Card:

Card Number: Expiration Date: Security Code:

☐ PO

Purchase Order Number:

StudySync Text Fulfillment, BookheadEd Learning, LLC
610 Daniel Young Drive | Sonoma, CA 95476